A
Mother's
Touch

Waldo Theus

WESTBOW
PRESS®
A DIVISION OF THOMAS NELSON
& ZONDERVAN

WestBow Press books may be ordered through booksellers or by contacting:

WestBow Press
A Division of Thomas Nelson & Zondervan
1663 Liberty Drive
Bloomington, IN 47403
www.westbowpress.com
844-714-3454

ISBN: 979-8-3850-1118-6 (sc)
ISBN: 979-8-3850-1119-3 (e)

Library of Congress Control Number: 2023920790

Print information available on the last page.

WestBow Press rev. date: 11/15/2023

Dedication

My book is dedicated to the memory and life of our mother.
Mr. Huetta Jackson Theus:

- A loving and, giving mother and grandmother.
- A mother who worked lived and sacrificed her life for her children, husband and family.
- A mother who was a friend and teacher to her family and everyone that knew her.
- Our mother didn't cry from the pain, she endured the last moments of her life.

She cried for the family she loved with all her mind, heart and soul but had to leave.

On July 17, 2009 at 11:37 am, our mother passed away from this world to the other side from bone cancer. After being released from her physical body in this world.

God allowed her to touch her son's shoulder before leaving. From her touch God blessed me to write the words, she couldn't speak during the last days of her life.

So that our mother's thoughts and words could be written and set free. To be shared with her husband, daughters, loved ones and the world.

After four years and sixty-eight spiritual letters totaling over thirty-one thousand words, our mother's book "A Mother's Touch" was completed.

Acknowledgments

My spiritual letters are written to God, who gave us life.
To our Mothers, which brought forth our life.
To my wife, family and friends which help me enjoy this life.
To anyone that desires to know God's and,
learn to do his will in their life.

Contents

Biography

Mrs. Huetta Theus was born January 2, 1941 in Bonita, Louisiana. She was the third oldest of eight children, born to her mother Mozell Bankston and her father Odell Johnson. Her parents, were born in different parts of Louisiana. A martial conflicts caused her parents to separate and, later divorced. After living with her mother for a few months after her divorce, Mozell decided to relocate her family to California. Her mother, Buella Bankston told her daughter she could take the two boys. But our mother and her sister Gene had to stay with her in Wilmot, Arkansas until she was settled. Mozell left for California in search of work and a new life. Not knowing her children would never be together again as a family. Mozell was never financially able or allowed to relocate her daughters to California.

Our mother and father met as teenagers, after his family relocated from Benedetti, Louisiana to Wilmot, Arkansas. They were attracted to each other but, she was in a relationship with a young man servicing in the army. Being our father's friend, he asked him to look after his girlfriend until he returned. He was killed a few years later while, serving in the Korean War.

It was during this time our great-grand father, Isaac Bankston hired our father to work on his farm. His parents Frank and, Arie Theus told him it was a good opportunity. With him and his brother Robert working, they could help support their three sisters Dolly, Betty and Janie. Learning to drive a tractor as a teenager, our father had no problem working on the farm. Increasing conflicts between my Uncle Robert and his father motived him to leave Arkansas. He relocated to California and later moved to Las Vegas to live.

After our parents started dating, our great-grandmother tried to keep them apart. Buella continued to make up false stories, about our father and, other women even after they were married. It's believed her actions were caused by her fear, of being alone after the death of her husband years earlier. Or, she didn't want to lose the granddaughter she loved and had raised for so many years.

Because of Buella actions and, our parent's martial conflicts they separated shortly after my sister Stephanie was born. Our father relocated to Las Vegas for a few years and lived with his brother Robert. Our mother remained in Wilmot and worked at a local nursing home. She continued her medical career for over thirty-five years until her retirement.

Our father sent money to make sure our mother, sister and I had what we needed. After two years, he relocated to Little Rock, Arkansas. While in Little Rock he lived with his youngest sister Janie and her husband James. He called our mother to let her know, he was working and living in Little Rock. After a number of visits to Wilmot, they decided to move their family to Little Rock. A year later we relocate to Little Rock, our mother started working at UAMC as a nurse's assistant. Our father worked at Colonial Bakers, as a production worker. Years later he was promoted to an eighteen wheeler driver.

During these years two additional sisters Ethel and Angela were born into the family.

A couple of years after Angela was born, our great-grandmother

Buella became ill with complications caused by her diabetes. Gene was alone with four children to care for. So our parents ask her to relocate to Little Rock and live with us. After living with us a few months her leg was amputated, Buella passed away from heart failure a year later. During the year Buella lived with us there were no conflicts between her and my parents. She wasn't criticized or blamed for her past words or actions.

She was our great-grandmother, who was shown respect every day of her life she lived with us.

It's Better to Let Them Go!
Than to Let Them Suffer!

"A Mother's Touch" was completed after four years and sixty-eight spiritual letters. Many of my spiritual letters written years ago are the first ones written in my book. This letter was written two years after our mother's death. It describes our mother leaving this world to be with God and our loved ones in heaven. After our mother's touch, God blessed me to walk through his spiritual door. And write these spiritual letters to my family, her loved ones and the world.

I've been told many times it's difficult to accept death. And understand God's will and purpose in our life. This has never been truer, than after the passing of a parent or loved one. Everything I learned as a child and experienced as an adult changed.

After our mother's death my:

- Mind, heart and soul grieved for the mother I loved.
- Belief in God changed, from him having all power to having no power.
- Belief and truth in God turned to anger.
- Faith in God passed away with my mother.

Her only suffering was being unable to see or, talk to her family before her death. Two years after her death, I began to see the weakness of my faith. I served God as an usher for years and, prayed daily for his grace, mercy and love in my life. But when I look back, I see good words and actions but a weak faith in God.

I remember telling others, "When your thoughts, become incon- sistent with our actions. Then you're lying and deceiving yourself!" Looking back, I remember lying and deceiving myself while asking God. Where are you? Why weren't you here to save my mother? What went wrong? I was asking God for a miracle but, my faith fought with God's will and purpose for our mother's life.

I wanted a miracle, "Like the one when Jesus raised Lazarus from the dead." (John 11:1-45, NIV). Like many loving children, I would have gladly given my life to take our mother's place. I couldn't stop thinking about her sacrifices and her labors of love. To provide her family, with what they needed to be happy. The sacrifices she and our father made working part-time jobs to provide for their children. Our parents rarely purchased anything for themselves. They took money from what they needed to make sure we had the clothes we needed for school. Now she laid before me, unable to talk or open her eyes. Because I couldn't do anything to help our mother, my thoughts filled with pain and anger. I knew she wouldn't have allowed me to take her place. But I wanted to do something, to help her. My father, sister and I did as she requested before going into the hospital. She requested that one of us remained at the hospital at all times. My first three nights back home were spent at the hospital. Which allowed my father and sisters to rest.

As the days passed I come to realize, it's better for a child to grieve for a parent. Then for a parent to grieve from the loss of a child. Filled with unanswered questions about our mother future, my thoughts filled with anger. I was angry with everyone, from the intensive care doctors to my family. I was angry with my mother for trusting a young intern to perform a medicinal procedure. Which may have contributed to her death. I was angry at myself, for not being able to do something to help her. When she needed me the most. The growing anger in my heart, had to give way to the love for my mother and family. Our mother was still here and she needed me to comfort her and my family.

I told her about my conversation with God, while driving from Dallas, TX to Little Rock, AR. In my conversation, "I told God my mother didn't need this amount of cleansing to enter heaven!" I told our mother, "Her suffering would put Job's suffering to shame!"

Being unable to talk, or open her eyes, she would smile with a "You think so!" expression. While turning her head and making a grunting sounds. Later in her illness I repeated another message God gave me a weeks earlier. God told me to tell my mother, "Whatever she was going through, would only last for a little while!" She continued to make grunting noises and moved her head. To let her family know she was still here and hadn't given up.

After receiving a bad cancer report from the doctors. I held our mother's hand during the last minutes of her life. In my pain and grief I had to accept two things. The first was God's will and purpose for our mother's life. Secondly, before going into ICU our mother requested no additional procedures or operations be performed to extend her life. Lying in her hospital bed during the last minutes of her life, our mother began to cry.

She didn't cry:

- Tears of fear.
- Tears pain.
- Because she was dying.

She cried tears of love for:

- The family she loved with all her heart and soul but had to leave.
- The life she enjoyed on this side.
- The words she wanted to say to her family before she left.

Our mother cried tears of joy to a God, she has known from childhood. She was now preparing to meet him face-to-face.
Glory!
Knowing her time on this side had ended, I told our loving mother the last words she would hear on this side. "You can rest now, "Sister Theus" it's alright your little while is over!" I didn't have to tell her everything that could be done had been done. She already knew that, my job was to stand between God's two worlds. Then help our mother and, her family say goodbye to each other.
As our loving mother's soul said goodbye:

- To her husband, our father said goodbye to his wife and soulmate.
- To her daughters, her daughters said goodbye to their mother.
- When our mother said goodbye to her son, her son had to say goodbye to his loving mother.

After being touched by one of God's angels. Our mother was free from her physical body and God's world. Because she couldn't speak before she left, God blessed her to do one thing. Before starting it journey toward heaven. With God's Holy Spirit and our mother's soul in his angel arms. God blessed our mother a second time. By allowing her to touch her son shoulder before leaving this side. After her touch occurred, I could feel the breeze from the angel wings. When it left, on its journey back to heaven. After touching my shoulder, I was blessed to write all the things our mother couldn't say before she left and more.
Her touched blessed me, to tell everyone God is real. Just as

she taught us! It allowed me to tell everyone, that feared death to know there's another side to our life.

The other side of our life:

- Can't be seen from this side.
- Can't be heard from this side.
- It can't be touched from this side.

But when we pass over to the other side, we're allowed to see the true beauty of God's worlds. We're blessed to see and feel God love all around us. Which can't truly be felt from this side of heaven. When we cross over, we're allowed to see God's angels. Descending on his world and freeing his most precious angels from their physical bodies. After our freedom from this side, God's love for us is revealed a million times the size of his universe.

In the last days of her life, our mother's only pains were being unable to see and talk to the family she loved. If she had remained on this side of heaven, as her family wanted. Her life would have been filled with pain doctor's appointments and, medicinal procedures. As much as it hurt us to lose our loving mother, as it would any family. It would have hurt us a thousand times over to see her suffer every day of her life. By remaining with us on this side. Knowing this it's better to let them go, to the other side. Than remain with us on this side and suffer in pain.

Paul knew this when he wrote:

- All things known and, unknown.
- All things seen and, unseen.
- All things work for the good of those, who love God.

Who are called, according to his will and, purpose in their life.
"And we know now all things God works for the good of those who love him, who have been called according to his purpose" (Roman 8:23, NIV).

With a sad but joyous heart, I have written our mother's thoughts, to her family and loved ones.

My hope is that, "A Mother's Touch" will help us realize what our loved ones wanted to say to us.

Before they left to be with God in heaven.

Crossing Over

I take joy in knowing, our mother has crossed over to the other side.

Our mother crossed over:

- In the arms of an angel.
- Knowing her life on this side was finished.
- Knowing the pain she endured, preparation her soul for her journey home to God.

While our mother was alive, she sacrificed all she had for her family and loved ones. "I am sending you out like sheep among wolves. Therefore, be as shrewd as snakes and, as innocent as doves." (Matthew 10:16, NIV)

While on our spiritual journey through life, God ask us to have the shrewdness of a snake and the heart of a dove.

With the shrewdness of a snake our mother:

- Wasn't deceived by the words, or actions of people.
- Raised her children to love God and, be their best.
- Loved and respected God will and, purpose for her life.

With the heart of a dove she loved everyone. Even those who didn't love themselves. She touched the hearts, spirits and souls of everyone she met. As we live the life God has blessed us to live. Our words and actions like our parents will say what we love. What does your words and actions saying about your life?

Have our words and actions been of:

- Peace or war!
- Love or hate!
- Offering to God!
- Or, offering to our pride and selfishness!

Are our words and, actions being said to build people up or to tear them down.

Isn't now is a good time to:

- Think about our words and, actions.
- Change our behavior.
- Ask our self, "How much longer do I have to live on this side?"

When we truthfully answer these questions, we begin preparing for our journey. We start looking up and forward, rather than looking down and backward. We start changing our words and actions rather than blaming others. When we truthfully look at our self, rather than the people, things and distractions around us. We grow in belief, faith and love because we're assured of one thing. Our day will come, when we will have to cross over to the other side!

When we cross over to the other side. We will choose to cross over:

- Willingly or unwillingly.
- In the joy of the Holy Spirit, or in pain.
- In the arms of an angel.

Or we'll choose to cross over surrounded by our fears, shame, pride and the dark angel.

Lastly, when we cross over to the other side.

We will choose to be in the arms of God angels or those of the dark angel!

To My Sisters

Let Us Not Forget!

L et us not forget!" and "It's Time!" are two of the three spiritual letters written to my sisters after our mother passed away. I waited and prayed for months. Before the thoughts of family members in unmarked graves touched my thoughts and heart.

Love and sacrifices, we all witness these words in action from our childhood. They were placed in our thoughts, hearts, and souls. They were placed on our bodies, when our parents saved nothing for themselves. Our parents shamed themselves with no money and, old clothes. So the children they loved, could have what they needed in life to be happy. Let us not shame our mother, with our words and actions. We can't allow the pain and, grief of our mother's death. To cause us to forget, what she taught us. We can't keep allowing our pain to control our thoughts, emotions or actions.

I don't care who did what, when, or why?

We all have enough on our plates, without allowing our emotional pains and the dark angel to divide us. For all we have lost, after our mother's death. Let us not hold onto the pain and anger left behind.

We can't allow our mother's:

- Smiles of joy and, love to be turned into faces of anger.
- Laughter be turned into sadness.
- Labors, tears and sacrifices of love, die by our actions or our lack of action.
- Make-up kisses be turned into words of anger, or actions of violence.

Life is too short to allow our negative thoughts and, actions to overcome our parents love for us. We have to allow the good thoughts, words, actions and memories of our mother. Heal our thoughts, pain and soul. We have to remove everything in our path, which blocks us from God and her love for us. We have to allow God to give us courage, strength during times of weakness, pain and anger.

When we do these things and, we can!

- We preserve the sacrifices, memories and love of our mother.
- We make God, our parents and loved ones smile with joy.
- We renewed our love for them daily through our words, actions and life.

When we do these things our hope and faith in God, will heal us through the grief and pain of her death.

Most of all, you don't want me to come to Arkansas upset! Because my conversation will only be one way.

"My way!"

Kiss and make-up, Remember!

We have to always remember, what our mother taught us to do before she left.

I love you all!!!!!!!!!

It's Time!

I t's time regardless of the:

- Lingering pains of grief we feel.
- Cost, or time which has passed.
- Drawing or words which are needed on our mother's memorial.

You and I both know what time it is! What we don't want is to:

- Not do, what we were taught.
- Not do, what our mother would have done for us.
- Think its ok, to wait a little longer.

What we don't want is to think there are too many decisions and problems to get anything done. Most of all, we don't want our mother to continue laying in an unmarked grave. My beloved sisters, we're looking at seven months. As difficult as it is we must do it for our mother and, for ourselves. We know the pain of our mother's death, will never leave our hearts or souls. But we must go forward with our life and the loving memories of our mother in our hearts.

We have to keep telling ourselves:

- Whatever it takes!
- Whatever the obstacles!
- Whatever the cost!

It's time, to honor our mother's life! By not letting anything stop us!

It's Our Responsibility!

T his is the final spiritual letter written, to my sisters seven months after our mother passing. It was past time to purchase a memorial for our mother. None of us were ready, but it had to be done! Being the oldest it was my job to help my sister purchase her memorial.

We have all suffered the loss of a loving mother, which we loved dearly. The loss of any mother or loved will always bring pain and grief. In time we will learn to accept our loss and, endure the pain and grief we feel. There are many stages ahead, which we will face individually and endure together. The last stage is accepting, God's will in our mother life. By saying goodbye to the mother we loved with all our heart. One of our stages is to select her memorial.

I emailed each of you twice, about her memorial last month. I know none of us are ready to hurt and feel the pain and, grief of her loss again. But we have to remember, none of us are alone in our loss. Or, the decisions we need to be make. We're together in what we think and how we feel. We must be together now concerning the decisions, which needs to be made about her memorial. Just as we were together at our mother bedside.

Only one reply to my e-mail, ok "No Prisoner's!"

Because I received one reply to my third e-mail about our mother's memorial. How about this e-mail!

We're too:

- Sad and, upset to understand each other's grief.
- Hurt, to forgive or accept each other's smallest mistakes.
- Overcome with pain and, grief to love our self or each other.

We're too upset with God to understand or accept his will and, purpose in our mother's life. But we each know, if she had lived as we wanted. Her daily pains would have killed each of us a thousand times over. Nothing stopped us from being by our mother's bedside. So we're not going to allow anything to stop us now. If we don't purchase her memorial, Who will? If it's not our responsibility, then whose responsibility is it? The pains we've suffered after our mother's death hasn't stopped us from living our life. Or doing what we needed to do for our self and family. Therefore nothing is going to stop us from purchasing and, installing a memorial honoring our mother's life. If for any reason you're not ready to purchase her memorial.

Its' okay, I understand! If you're unable to help, all I have to say is "Don't get in my way!"

Because if I have to bring a memorial 360 miles from Dallas, TX to Little Rock, AR. That's what I am going to do. I want allow our mother to continue laying in an unmarked grave, like other family members.

I won't allow it and neither should you!

No reply is needed to this e-mail and no future e-mails will be forwarded concerning this subject.

A Thank You to My Sisters

I want to thank each of you for your courage and sacrifices of love. Thank you for enduring the decisions, we needed to make for ourselves and, our mother. Thank you for the pain and grief you over came to honor our mother's life. Our parents gave us more than just food, clothes and shelter. They gave us there:

- Compassion, disciple and determination.
- Passion to live and, enjoy life.
- Hearts, souls and love.

They gave us their wisdom of this world and, a love of God. For all they gave us, the only thing they ask for. Is the respect a child should give a loving parent. By marking the completion of our mother's life journey on this side. We have honored our mother's life and healed our hearts and souls. Our sacrifices of love has let her know, how much we truly love her. As we continue our daily journey toward our mother, family members and loved ones.

We do what they taught us to do:

- We love God.
- We love our self.
- We love our Families.

We're grateful for the love our parents and, loved ones gave us while they were alive.

Their love and lives were a gift of God's grace, mercy and love to us!

My Sister's Spirit

My three sisters, have the spirit of an angel. They have the spiritual beautiful and soul of our mother.

You're all covered in our mother's presence from your:

- Hair to our face.
- Shoulder to your legs.
- Skin complexion to you spirit.

Our knowledge and wisdom are touched by the memories of her words.

As we travel daily, toward our mother:

- A wonderful part of her is always with us.
- Her words and, soul will comfort us.
- The spirit of God's "Trinity" is with us.

Your words of love and, your actions of faith honors God and, our parents daily. After purchasing the memorial, which will marks the resting place of our loving mother. We have mark the resting place of a great and wonderful mother. She made mistakes as we all will! But we witness her persevere through her mistakes. We witness our mother live a good and happy life. Having to discipline us, hurt her more than it did us. Some of us "Like me!" needed more discipline. After standing proud and strong in the worst situations. We witness our mother love for her family, loved ones and co-workers.

Like our mother:

- We have endured your mistakes and, consequences.
- We enjoy a happy life, based on your faith.
- We are a copy of a loving God and, our mother's love.

Like our mother we stood proud and, strong in bad situations. Your families and loved ones witness your faith and love. Regardless of the things we will lose as you journey toward God, our mothers and loved ones.

Our mother's and, loved ones:

- Smiles, joy and laughter want be one of them.
- Beautiful spirit and, soul want be one of them.
- Love for God and, us want be one of them.

We are filled with joy and happiness as we journey toward God and, our mother. The distance which separate us, want allow us to be together daily. But our thoughts and hearts will always be together in love. Even with hundreds of miles between us, our spirits and souls are together in love. When we struggle with the challenges and pains of life. The Holy Spirit, our faith and our love for each other bonded us together in love. God and, our faith will help us endure the pains of life. In our journey toward God and, our loved ones. Each of us will reach our heavenly destination at different time. We know our love for each other will remain, even after we've reach the gates of heaven. Journey in peace, joy and, love my beloved sister's!

Until we're together again, in the presence of God and our parents.

What a Beautiful Day!

When the hot temperatures and days of summer begin to disappear. The cooler days of autumn arrive on a beautiful and cloudy morning. No longer distracted by the heat of summer the skies are cloudy and the weather is cool. The birds fly high in the sky, rather than below the trees. As they did during the heat of summer.

Looking up:

- The sky looks like, an enormous blue ocean.
- The sunlight covers the clouds, like a blanket.
- Hundreds of angel shaped clouds, were drifting across the sky.

With autumn continuing its approach toward us, the seasonal changes of fall been to occur. Looking around, I see new grass growing from under dead grass left behind from the summer heat. As the Holy Spirit touched my soul, I realize only God's power and love could have created such a peaceful and beauty world.

As I continued to look around:

- Hundreds of brown leaves, were laying on top of the new grass.
- The birds were using the dead grass to rebuild their nest. For their young and, the approaching winter season.
- The squirrels were storing up acorns for winter.

Months later, the angel shaped clouds begin rushed away as if they were running. After autumns completes another seasonal cycle, fall begins to arrive. God blesses us to enjoy the beauty of our life in similar life cycles.

In the spring of our youth we enjoy:

- The challenges of growing and, learning about life and the world around us.
- The beauty of our family, friends and school.
- The pleasures of romance and, love.
- Our growing belief and, faith in God.

But when the harsh temperatures of summer, approaches the adult cycle of our life some of our joy is lost.

When we grow into adults we:

- See the ugly reality of life and, God's world.
- Receive numerous challenges from our families, friends and educational standards.
- Regent and, hate the ones we once loved because of their deceit and lies.
- Witness our belief and, faith in God fight with his will and purpose for our life.

We feel burdened by a life we neither choose, ask for nor wanted. After God blesses us to enter the mature autumn and fall cycles of our life. We understand the mistakes, challenges and lessons of our youth. We learn to accept and embrace the good and bad in our self, others and God's world. We allow our faith in God's Holy Spirit to comfort us. Through the challenges we face from our family members, friends and school.

More importantly, we learned to embrace those that hurt and disappointed us in life. We refuse to carry their pains, grief and the burdens of their lives forward with us. We don't allow those lost in the darkness of pride, anger and sin to cause us to be the same way. We know:

- The final winter season in our life, awaits our arrival.
- There's nothing we can do to prevent its arrival.
- Our faith and, the Holy Spirit is with us until the final season arrives in our life.

The loss of our loved ones and, friends is evidence of the final season which lies ahead. Knowing the final season in our life is traveling toward us.

We no longer have time to waste on:

- Foolish thoughts, words or emotions.
- Unachieved wants, goals or dreams.
- Childish things and people lost in darkness.

Knowing our youthful seasons are behind us. We're compiled to go forward with whatever God has blessed us with on our journey thought life. Whatever skills, knowledge, wisdom, hope and faith God has blessed us to acquire on our journey. We carry them forward with us.

As we travel forward in life:

- We have to be like the new grass, we must grow from under the dead things in our life.
- We don't allow hundreds of challenges and, problems to lay on top of our life.
- We do as the birds have done, we build for our future and those of our children.
- We do like the squirrels, we store up money blessing and, faith for the storms which lay ahead.

Like the angel shaped clouds, we rush to God and our loved ones. Before problems and, storms come into our life. Before the final season arrives in our life.

We enjoy every:

- Thing, each day has to offer.
- Minute, with our loved ones.
- Day, God blesses us to live.

We enjoy the beautiful memories of loved ones. Which are no longer with us on this side. Most of all we enjoy the beautiful life, and family God has blessed us with. Because we realize, the final season in our life will arrive soon enough.

Without us looking for it!

Watching Dreams Fade Away

T his spiritual letter was written to my sisters, for the sacrifices of love they made for our mother and their family.

The things you wanted and dreamed for in your life weren't failures. They were sacrifices of love you made for the ones you love and, who loves you. When you look back at the things you didn't achieve or couldn't have in life.

You didn't fail!

Situations and, events beyond your control made it appear you didn't succeed. Even after making the right decisions, the outcome wasn't what you expected or wanted. After sacrificing your wants and dreams for your loved ones and family members. You had to watch many of your dreams fade away. Which prevented you from achieving everything you wanted in life. But don't think for a minute your time, labors and sacrifices achieved nothing.

Don't allow yourself to:

- Think your sacrifices of love, had no rewards.
- Believe, or accept someone saying you failed.
- Measure your worth and life by what you didn't achieve or don't have.

Measure your worth and life by what you have done for those you love. Continually ask God to help you on your journey. Allow your faith time to deliver your request and prayers. If you don't allow your faith time to deliver your request and prayers. You will look around and become distracted by the people and, things of God's world. When you allow the people and things of God's world to distract you. They will block your path to your faith in God and, your joy and happiness on this side.

As difficult as it is to accept, be grateful for whatever earthly treasures are in your life. Continue to tell yourself, you didn't fail! Because you didn't given up or stop trying! While you're moving forward in life. Let your heart and soul find joy in the dreams and goals which hasn't faded away.

When you do this and, you can!

You're at peace with everybody and, everything on this side of heaven. You know from "A Mother's Touch" your eternal rewards aren't on this side anyway! We receive those rewards from God, after we have crossed over. To see our loved ones on the other side. Cling to your dreams and, your faith by thanking God daily for his blessing of life. Let your soul rest in the rewards of your efforts. And in the sacrifices of love you made like our loving mother and loved ones.

You didn't fail, "My Beloved Sisters!"

You sacrificed your wants and dreams for the betterment of yourself, family and loved ones. As our parents taught us to do! Like our parents, your actions, efforts and faith. Has allowed God to write your name in his, "Book of Life". When some of your dreams fade away, you know it's only "For a little While!"

We only have to endure the challenges and pains of this life "Just for a little While!"

With love to my, "My Beloved Sisters!"

Call My Name

"Call all my name" is a spiritual letter written about my childhood. It was written November 2010, 14 months after our mother passed away. It's a flash back to memories of a good and, wonderful childhood. When I wasn't good or wonderful! Our mother would continually called my name in her efforts to find me. I wouldn't answer her because, I was usually doing something bad which was going to get me into trouble. Knowing our mother, I knew I didn't have long, before she found me. So I would hurry to finish what I was doing before she found me.

Except, when I hurt myself! I would ran to my mother calling her name for help. There was a punishments and, consequences to face when I didn't answer and she found me. She would first correct my behavior, then I had to answer for my actions for not answering her call. Our mother had her own unique way of letting me know I was wrong. I knew her punishment wasn't far away. When I was bad, she would warn me with a long stare. But if my actions were serious, her hand and body movements would let me know. I was in serious trouble. She would confirmed my punishment, with the worst words I wanted to hear. "I am going to get you, when we get home!"

I believe the same statement is true of God, when we don't do as he ask! He continually calls our name throughout our life. But we ignored God and continue doing what we want, how we want, when we want. Then we rush to finish before the consequences of our words and, actions catch up with us. The minutes I experienced hiding as a child, adds up to years in our life. We find ourselves ignoring God for years until we're hurt, in pain or death touches our life. Then we pray a servant's prayer and run to God calling his name. Like a loving parents, God is there! With mercy, grace, understanding and love to remind us of the consequences of our words and actions.

My father would only call my name once. Then he would wait for me to arrive home. Our father was the talker in the family, he didn't believe in physical punishment except in extreme cases. He would talk to me, for what seemed like hours. If I interrupted him, he would start over where he stopped him or at the beginning of his statement. He would talk so long it became unbearable. I almost wished he would physically punish me and, get it over with. But if I was smart, it was better to seat and listen. Rather than risking the physical punishment of my father.

God reminds me of my earthly parents, after waiting for years for us, to listen to his Holy Spirit. He may choose to just listen to us and, do nothing. Until we received and accept his message of love. To surrender our will and, life over to him. God want reward us for unholy words or actions. That temporary reward comes from the dark angel. We may get tired of listing to the Holy Spirit talk to us. Like me, doing my childhood with my father. But we couldn't endure the loss of God's grace, mercy, love or his Holy Spirit in our life. Therefore, in the future, I suggest; "When we heard God calling our name!" We answer his call!

Before he decides to stop calling our name!

$\mathcal{J}$

See What You Have Done!

Being the oldest our parents made me responsible. For taking care of my sisters and the household when they were away. They would worked part-time jobs to earn extra money for the family. I was ask to finish the cooking do housework and, take care of my three sister's. I learned to do their hair, cooking and iron our clothes for school. My position occasionally cause conflicts with my oldest sister Stephanie.

Growing up our mother's love taught us to take care of our self and family members. When Stephanie and my conflicts escalated to physical confrontations, our mother had two punishments which she administered. The first was a physical punishment for harming each other. The second punishment was worst, we had to kiss each other on the cheek and make up. I remember Stephanie and me looking into each other eyes and, thinking "See what you have done!" After looking at each other, we would turned and, look at our mother. Her facial expressions let us know her first punishment would be repeated if we didn't do as she ask. With that being our motivation, we would approached each other with our eyes closed.

To prevent from having to look at each other. Then we take turns kissing each other on the cheek, hating every minute. As an added punishment for harming each other, we were sent to bed without dinner. This was our mother's punishments for her children, throughout our childhood. Regardless of the person or reason, whenever we harmed each other physically or emotionally we were taught to make up. Our childhood kiss on the cheek, changed into an apology when we grew older. It was years later, before I understand our mother's reasons for making us kiss each other on the cheek and make up.

She and, her sister Gene were separated from their mother and, family during their childhood. During their separation two additional sisters and brothers were born to her family. Years later when her mother tried to bring the family together. A conflict developed between her and her mother, which permanently separated the family. Our mother and Gene being separated from their family, caused them to develop emotional issues throughout their lives. They suffered from rejection issues, which weren't resolved until the last fifteen years of her life. These issues, along with interior conflicts created a void in their lives. Our mother nor Gene, were never close to their mother, four brothers and two sisters. During the last fifteen years of her life. She had an opportunity to see and meet all her brothers and sisters at their mother's funeral in California.

Years before her mother's funeral, I met my Aunt Mary in San Diego, CA in 1980. I was in California, playing football with S.M.U. in the Holiday Bowl against BYU.

During her fifteen years with her brothers and sisters. She renewed family bonds she never had in her life. Her renewed relationships with her brothers and, sisters helped me understand why our mother made us kiss and make up. She was teaching us to have an emotional bond. Which would help us though conflicts and, issues which could separate us. Our mother was teaching us to not let anyone, or anything separate you from your family. "Those who don't learn from the past are doomed to repeat it!"

Now that our loving mother is gone we:

- Understand our childhood punishment.
- See the acts of love in her words and actions.
- Realize how much, we miss the sound of her voice calling my name.

I miss her wonderful words, of wisdom and love. My grief and pain helps me remember our mother life with joy and love. We honor our mothers' life by sharing her teaching and, sacrifices of love with our families. Her words, actions and sacrifices symbolizes her love for God, her family and life. Everything good, bad, past and present are touched with God and our mothers' love.

They're in our life and, soul forever! Take care of yourself, I love you all!

Fear, Pain and Love

This spiritual letter was written November 20, 2009, on my sister Stephanie birthday. Our fears, pains, emotions and love are tools, used in spiritual warfare. God allows our fears, pain and love to help us on our journey in life.

God uses our fear to:

- Show us our weakness and, his path to heaven.
- Teach and, guide us in his will and, purpose in life.
- Discipline our understanding, belief and faith.

Our faith and, love for God helps us endure the fears and pains of life. Through our fears God allows the dark angel to:

- Darken our path and, life.
- Deceive our faith with pride.
- Test our faith and, love in him.

Our faith in God is the light, which guides our in journey. The pains, challenges and, problems of life are too numerous to count. In my childhood, the pains and problems of life starts out as small physical cuts. When I grew into an adults the pains and, problems of life begin to cuts into our thoughts and heart. When God calls, our loved ones home to heaven. The pains and grief of their death cuts into the deepest part of our spirit and soul. Pain and, fear forces us to embrace God's mercy, grace and love for our life. Or, our stubbiness and pride. God uses the pain of our loved ones loss. To free us from our self and, the things of his world. The loss of our love ones help us realize, "Where there is a great love for someone, pain and fear are there to challenge our faith and love in God."

When we're upset and, angry with God's will and purpose for our life. We allow the dark angel to uses our fear and, pain to challenge our faith and love for God. Our weak faith, fears and emotional pains, allows the dark angel permission to attack our thoughts, faith, soul and life. During his attack, we stop thinking our life and God's world is under our control. We endure the dark angel attack only through our belief in God's grace, mercy and love in our life. Our fears and, pains helps us accept God salvation for our life.

"And now these three remain faith, hope, and love. But the greatest of these is love (1 Corinthians 13:13 NIV).

As we journey towards heaven the fears and, pains of life will always be with us. The Holy Spirit will comforts us with hope and faith to endure them. On our journey toward heaven we know, what we can't see, touch or hear on this side. Has to be replaced by our faith in God. We come to realize our thoughts, emotions and actions have to surrender to a loving God.

We take comfort in knowing:

- The Holy Spirit is in us.
- The dark angel, has no power.
- Unless, God or we give it to him.

We know the love ones we lost and miss on this side. Are waiting for us on the other side. Isn't now a good time to ask our self, "What do we allow to control our fears, pains and love?"

Our belief, faith and love for God should answer this question for us! If it doesn't, the dark angel is waiting to help us answer it!

My Mother Told Me

My mother told me, started out as a spiritual song. I wrote it to sing during difficult times at work and in my life. It's about my parents teaching a young teenager to accept God's will, purpose and love in his life. It's like many of the spiritual letters in my book. They're the total essence of my parents teaching, faith and love in my life.

My parents told me there would be good times and, some would be bad. They continued to tell me, I would have to endure. Because my good days and, bad days will only last for a little while. They kept telling me to call on God, if I wanted to endure my little while and be free. They continually told me to not truth myself but, depend on God throughout my life. He would always be by my side, if I just called on his name.

But I was young and filled with prideful and a rebellious spirit. I didn't want anyone, to be by my side. My mother continued to tell me about God's love and mercy. But I would tell her, God didn't understand all the things in my life. They continued to tell me as a good parents should but, my thoughts wouldn't let me understand. After my parents love and, spirit touched my heart. I begin to listen as a son should. But my thoughts and, actions kept getting in my way. But as the years passed my words thanked God. For my parent's words of faith and love in my life. My heart was opened and, now my eyes could see God's true love for me. After I surrendered to God's holy will, I wrote my parents this song thanking them for doing God's will. I thanked God and, my parents for being in my life. This song and, my faith are all I could do. To let God and my parents know they were in my heart and soul.

Forever!

May God and these words add faith, strength and courage in your journey through out your life.

Time is Like a Silent Breeze!

I wrote this spiritual letter in July 2013. To honor the (4) year anniversary of my mother and, Marti's' passing. "Time is like a silent breeze!" I made this statement to a co-worker, concerning the four years anniversary of my mother and, Marti. The former A.V.P of our department passing. I acknowledged, how quickly the last four years has passed. By the time we realized four years had passed it was already gone.

When I realized, the silent breezes of their life had arrived:

- Four years had passed.
- The pain, grief and loneliness were hidden.
- Their memories, were stored away in my soul.

There precious thoughts and, memories had moved. From my present to my past and, from our thoughts to my soul. When these silent breezes of time and, love passed through my life. They leave behind, a timeless pain.

When these timeless breezes of pain and, love touches me:

- My thoughts cries out in pain, loneliness and anger.
- My dreams in life, fade away for a moment.
- My heart and, soul stands still in grief.
- I stop looking around and, start looking up.

To God wanting an answer to my pain, loss and anger. My heart and, soul fights to not surrender to God's will and purpose for their lives. But my grief and pain forces me to surrender to God's love. After surrendering to God, I realize he has answered my questions. He answers my pain and grief with their loving memories. After the beautiful memories my mother and friend flows from his Holy Spirit to my hearts and soul.

The pain of their loss is replaced with a tearful memories of joy and love. The Holy Spirit transforms the bitter taste of their death into joy. After looking through our faith, we realizing he has answered our questions. Through his Holy Spirit, God has healed our pain and, loneliness with their loving memory.

Every reminding us:

- God hears our cries.
- God knows and, understands our pain and grief.
- God loves us.

God is the master and, through our faith we're his humble servants that he loves unconditionally. The memories of our parents and, loved ones remind us, how short life is on this side. But the short life we live on this side is replaced with an eternity life on the other side. Our pain and loneliness on this side is replaced with a joyous family reunion on the other side. God has promised he will be with us, in us and above us. Until we reach him and, our loved ones in heaven. But until that day comes and, we see God and our loved ones again.

We must remember:

- Whatever thoughts, feeling, and storms you're going through. They'll only last for a "little while"
- Whatever issues, pains and bills we're dealing with on this side. Will only last for a "little while."

Because we know everything on this side is temporary. Don't allow:

- People and, things of his world to upset you.
- Our self, to get lost in the darkness of his world.
- Pain, anger or hatred, to steal the precious time God has given us.

We have to enjoy every minute of life, we have on this side! Because one day,

"The loving memories of our life, will be sent by God's Holy Spirit to our loved ones on this side!"

Take care of our stubborn father, until I come home! Then you'll have two problems to take care of!

I miss and Love you all! Your brother, Waldo!

Our Mother's Love

Our mother's love, was written six months after our mother passed away. It's a son describing his mother's character and, life to her family, friends and the world. It was written, to let everyone know the beauty of our mother spirit and soul. The wonderful loving heart she shared with everyone she met. No one will ever come close to matching our mother's beauty, or her spirit of love.

Our mother's:

- Hair was like, black silk.
- Face was like, an angel.
- Eyes were as bright and, beautiful as the moon.
- Heart was like, a dove.

In her youth and, much of her life her body was like a goddess. Her beautiful soul could only be matched by God's Holy Spirit. Our mother's character and heart were as big as a mountain. Her spirit of love, for everyone around her could fill the sky. She always gave her best, to her family and everyone she met. To the point of having nothing left for herself. The only thing she ask for, is the respect a child should give to a loving mother. And on Mother's

Day, her family give her a small present. As a symbol of gratitude and love for her years of labor, sacrifice and love.

When we look back, over the years our mother was with us. Then forward, to the years we'll be without her. The pain of her loss, will never leave our hearts and souls. Because of our mother's love, we smile at the past and the future. Our thoughts, hearts and souls will always be close to our mother. Her spirit of love is always with us, as we journey toward her daily. We know our mother is waiting for us, in heaven. With a smile, open arm, a hug and a kiss. Until our day comes to join her and our loved ones. We continue to do what she taught us, when she was alive.

We continue to:

- Thank and, praise God for our life.
- Take care of our self.
- Take care of our families and, loved ones.

If he wants it or not! We will continue to take care of our loving father.

Most of all we continue to take care of each other, with the same spirit of love that she taught us!

Little While

God has blesses us with a little while, to enjoy our life on this side! As difficult as it is to accept, we learn to accept our little while with joy. Unknowingly, we hide our little while in the back of our minds.

To help us forget, our little while:

- We fill our life with family, work and things to do.
- We use the people of his world as excuses for our actions.
- We use the things of his world as distractions.

We distract our self, by making the same mistakes in different ways. Regardless of what we do, there's no escaping or forgetting our little while in life.

Our little while on this side is like:

- A raging river, coming toward us.
- A tornado, with all the winds of time pushing ageist our life.
- A bolt of lightning, heading directly toward us.
- A comet, after traveled millions of miles it has reached its final destination.

While we have time we enjoy every:

- Day, as if it was our last.
- Sunrise, as if it's the last one we'll see.
- Member of our family, like it's the last time we'll see them on this side.

We don't waste the precious time God has given us, on foolish people or things. For those who think there little while want come.

Good luck with that!

They have choose to journey in darkness, without God's Holy Spirit or angels to guide them. They will journey in doubt, fear and pain. They think they don't need God's mercy, love or his Holy Spirit on their journey. Unlike those that are lost in darkness, we have to stop and ask our self. Why enjoy the rewards of this life for a little while. Then make decisions which will cause us to suffer for eternity in the darkness of hell. Why obey God for a little while and, then turn away from him when our life is ending. Why do we think and act like our life on this side want end. When our loved ones, have already crossed over to be with God.

Don't let the foolish knowledge and, wisdom of his world. Deceive you and keep you a prisoner to darkness. We must allow our belief and, faith in God to lift us above our pride and the foolish wisdom of his world. We take joy in knowing we only have a little while to enjoy the earthly life which God has given us.

Before we choose to spend eternity with God and, our loved ones in heaven!

If we choose, there's always another option!

Just for a Little While!

This spiritual letter was written, a few weeks after our mother passed away to the other side. My sisters read the original version, which was written years ago. But what they didn't see were the four re-visions, I made in the past two years. The final draft is so touching it still begins tears to my eyes. It's a small example of how our mother and, loved ones memory and essences remains in our thoughts, soul and life.

Just for a little while our mother was with us:

- Her love put us to sleep every night.
- Her love was there, to wake us every morning.
- Her smile made us happy.
- Her laughter made us smile.

For all the years our mother was in our lives. It feels like, it was just for a little while. While we're on this side of heaven!

We must endure the last:

- Words from her lips.
- Sight of her face
- Touch of her embrace.

We must endure the last of so many things, we thought would never end. With a sad heart and soul we journey toward our mother daily. Knowing the one we loved the most in our life is somewhere ahead of us.

She's too:

- Far to be seen.
- Far to be heard.
- Far to touched.

But our mother's loving spirit, is close enough to be felt in our hearts. Her beautiful spirit and life is close enough, to be felt in the deepest parts of our soul.

We know our mother is waiting for us in heaven:

- With a smile.
- With a hug.
- With a kiss of love.

She's waiting on our arrival to be with God, her and our loved ones. I pray that we allow God, to bless us with hope, faith and love. Every day of our journey, toward the mother we loved. And, who loved us with all her heart and soul.

To our mother: Mrs. Huetta Theus From your children: Waldo, Stephanie, Ethel and Angela.

An Unmeasurable Love

Written on the 5 years anniversary, of our mother's passing. When another anniversary arrives and passes, the unmeasurable love of our mother and, loved ones touches our heart. It's an unmeasured love of actions and sacrifices rather than empty words and no action.

It's an unmeasured love of:

- Sacrifices, rather than pride.
- Labors, rather than selfish wants and desires.
- Disciple and, respect rather than criticism and threats.

Our mother's words of love, gave us encouragement and construc- tive thoughts. The purity of her love, will continue to live in our hearts and soul forever.

God and, time has removed her:

- Words for our ears.
- Face from our presence.
- Loving touch from our lives.

We can't be sad too long, for those we have lost. We learn to be happy for their life and the memories we shared with them. Our parents and, loved ones were earthy treasures which God blessed us to enjoy. When the pains of this day touches, our thoughts and hearts. Allow the love of God and, our mother to touch our soul.

When the memories of this day:

- Fill us with pain, anger and sadness. Allow God and, their loving memoires to wash them away.
- Make us question God's will, purpose and love in their lives. We know their pains in this life are over.

They're with God and, their loved ones and, "They don't want to return to this side!" Neither will we, after we have crossed over to be with God and our loved ones. We have to allow the memories and life of our loved ones to renew our thoughts, hearts and souls. When we rejoice in their life, rather than in the pains and grief of their death. We allow our soul to move another step closer to God and their spirit in heaven.

We're another step closer to:

- Our heavenly home.
- Their words of love.
- Seeing God and, being with them.

Until our day of freedom comes, we wait in faith and love and live a life filled with joy and happiness.

Journey in peace and, love until God ends our "Little while" on this side.

To be free for eternity with them!

Waldo Theus

Written July 17, 2014

To Our Father

To Our Father

You have always been what God, wanted a men to be to his family. You provided our needs, while sacrificing your wants.

You and our mother sacrificed your lives to make your children and family happy.

No amount of words can describe or measure the love. You and our mother gave to your children and extended families.

My words can't match the years of labor and love you gave to us. Therefore, I am writing these spiritual letters as a thank you.

For everything you did to make us feel loved and happy. You and, our mother were truly one of a kind!

Thank You for Being There!

From the beginning of our lives you and, our mother were there to care for us. When my sister and I were without knowledge, you taught us understanding and took care of us. You protected us when we were weak and, feed us when we were hungry. You guided us in our first steps and, were there to pick us up when we fell. You taught us about God's love and how to be kind and, caring to everyone. Even if they tried to take advantage of us. You showed us strength, love, and gave us beautiful memories. Which we'll remember for forever. Regardless of what you or our mother think you didn't do as parents.

Take joy in knowing:

- You did your best!
- You taught us knowledge and, wisdom.
- You sacrificed your lives, for your children.
- You taught us, to respect and love God and our self.

By respecting others, if they deserved it or not. You continued to love us, with all your heart and soul. Regardless of our words or actions. Thank you for your sacrifices of love, you gave to us for so many years. You and our mother could have done anything with you lives. But you chose to sacrifice your lives, for the children and, family you loved. For all you have done, all I can say is thank you!

Knowing all the beauty places you could have visited and lived.

You returned to Arkansas to raise the children you loved.

Thank you!

Because of the time, efforts and money you sacrificed to take care of us. Thank you!

For all the times you should have punished, my bad sisters and didn't. Thank you!

Because, I deserved twice their punishment. For all the times your love and, wisdom helped me with my pride and anger.

Thank you!

Take pride in knowing your actions of love, like our mother's will live on for generations to come. Through a new generation, which God has allow you to see and touch.

Thank you is too small a word. To describe all you and, our mother did for your family. So take pride and, joy in knowing my words come from the thoughts, hearts and souls of your love. For the years of sacrifices, care and love you gave your children, families and friends.

I pray, when the time comes you will allow us to take care of you! With the same spirit of love!

You Weren't Forgotten!

Your sacrifices of love will endure for years. After the minutes and, hours of this Father's Day has passed. Your years of sacrifices and, actions of love prevent you from having to say many words. When times got hard, you worked even harder to make sure the family you loved had what they needed to be happy. When God called your wife and, our mother to heaven. You allowed God's spirit of love to touch your soul with tears of grief, joy and love.

You showed us:

- An inner strength from God.
- How to cry and, smile at pain with joy.
- To not fear the unknowns of death.

You taught us faith in an unknown future, without our mother. You let us know, God has a better world on the other side. When we look back in love at the loved ones we lost. We cherish their life and, the times we share with them on this side.

My letter is a thank you, for all the Father's Day's you didn't receive a gift. But your love and, patience was always there as our gift. This spiritual letter is a reminder of the gifts you wanted but, didn't receive in life.

They'll be rewarded to you in heaven.

It's a reminder that you and our mother are a blessing from God. We thank God for placing both of you in our lives!

Our Father's Light

After the pasting of another birthday, our father's light is going dim. As years pass we see their effects on his mind, body and soul. Without our mother here to comfort him. He's comforted by God, us and her loving memories. We're blessed and happy for all the years our father has been with us. But we realize his journey is coming to an end.

Like all our journeys will one day!

I am saddened by each passing day, I am not at his side. We know one day we'll be by his side for the last time. The Holy Spirit is prepared his body and, soul to join our loving mother and family members on the other side.

While our loving father is still here with us:

- We spend every minute, in his presence.
- We enjoy every time, he calls our name.
- We enjoy every day, we see and touch his face.

We do everything we can to make our father life happy. Our parent's labors of love and sacrifices date back to our childhood. Our labors of love is to help our father in their journey back to God, his wife and loved ones. Their sacrifices of love made us happy, even during the bad times in life. Our parent's labors and sacrifices of love are visual proof of God's humble servants. There's nothing we can do to stop our father's journey toward God and our mother. The thought of his leaving, saddens our hearts and souls. Like our loving mother, he has always been a great father.

He isn't a man:

- Of words, he's a man of action.
- That complains about people and problems.
- That rejected God, he taught us how to do God's will!

He's a man that love God, worked hard and taught his children to do the same thing. For the love you've given us for so many years.

We only have a:

- Few gifts of love, to show you our gratitude.
- Few dollars, to help you with bills and food.
- Smile, kiss and hug to comfort your loneliness.

We can only attempt, to return the love you given us for so many years. Looking back at my last visit, I remember the proud words you told my sisters and me before I left. "You thanked God and our mother for providing you with such good and caring children to take care of you!"

You never said:

- A word about your years of labors and sacrifices.
- We owned you a dollar, for all the thousands of dollars you spent on us.
- Negative statements, or criticized us for our mistakes.

You would always say;

"Well, now you know for yourself! Now that you've experienced it for yourself. No one has to tell you what mistakes you made!"

We realize, you were both sent to us by God! We have always seen God's spirit of love in your words, actions and life. I wasn't there, to help our mother when she became illness. But you know we'll be by your bedside, when you need us! Just as we were by our mother's bedside before she left.

Take care of our loving father, until I come home to visit. Stay by his side as we were by our mother side. Like our loving mother, our father want permit any procedures to extend his life on this side. Like us he misses his wife, soul mate and friend.

He will never see again, on this side.

Like us our father has a hole in his soul, which can't be filled by anything on this side of heaven. Like our mother we rejoice in his presence and, the sight of your face. We're happy at the sounds of his voice, which is still allowed to call our name.

We're blessed by the godly life, you have lived before God, your children and loved ones.

No man, or woman knows the hour or day when God's angel, will come to touch their soul!

May the peace, joy and love of God be with us until our touch occurs!

To My Wife

Tina

These spiritual letters are written to my wonderful wife, Tina. They're written because of her beautiful spirit, which is like my mother's.

I wrote them, because of my love for her and her love for me. Many of my letters were written, while Tina and I were dating.

I wrote them to share my humor, love and my plans for our future together.

If I May?

If I may?
I would like to tell you how I feel about for you.
I want you to know:

- I was weak, but you made my spirit stronger.
- I was unsure, but your love gave me the courage to endure.
- I was upset, but your spirit calmed my heart and soul.

I lost faith today, but your faith in God gave me the hope and strength to not give up.
Though we are apart, my spirit is with you:

- My mind thinks of you continually.
- My heart is filled with joy at your presence.
- God has touched our spirits and, souls to be united in faith and love.

The challenges and storms in our life will makes us stronger in understanding, wisdom and our faith in God.
I pray for God's blessing on our relationship, families and every day of our lives together.

It's Time to Go!

H ello my love!
I am sending you this e-mail to inform you of my plans to leave work at 3:30pm today. Please have your bags, books, papers and other personal items ready to go at this time. No additional e-mails will be forwarded, to remind you of our departure time. If my request isn't accepted, you will receive a phone call from me on the toll way. My phone call will inform you, that you'll need alternative transportation for your ride home today. If we need to discuss my e-mail please feel free to do so when you arrive home. As you read my e-mail please remember how much I love you and, need you in the car before I leave.

Please remember my thoughtful words concerning your personal items and our departure time. Please remember the loving phone call I offered to make from the toll way to check on you. And, don't forget about my kind words concerning alternative transportation if you're not ready at 3:30.

With a loving heart I want to remind you, we can talk about any issue which may upsets you. My words and, actions are evidence of my love for you today and always.

"So don't be late!"

With love and humor, Waldo Theus

Don't Eat the Cornbread!

This letter shares my humor after cooking cornbread for my wife. As teenagers our mother taught each of her children how to cook. Being the oldest I finished and, prepared a number of meals for my sister, me and my parents. My love for cooking has continued throughout my life. But like our mother I have one problem! "I always burnt the bread!" It didn't matter what type, kind or style of bread it was, I would always burn it.

I am forwarding this e-mail to you as a warning! This warning relieves me of any liability, criticizing or stomach discomfort which you may experience. I have taken pre-cautions in the event a stomach problem occurs.

To make sure your family is informed:

- This e-mail is being forwarded to them.
- The phone numbers of a local emergency rooms, is included in my e-mal.
- The contact numbers for your doctor and pastor, was included in an attachment.

To ensure medical personal, know what you digested:

- A list of cornbread ingredients is on the counter.
- The quantities of each ingredient is included.
- The cooking instruction, I used is the bottom of the list.

After forwarding my warning e-mails and, the information listed above.

I only have, one thing left to say. "Don't eat the cornbread!"

With love and humor your husband, Waldo Theus

It's You!

When I woke up this morning:

- Your face was on my mind.
- Your smile was in my thoughts.
- The thoughts of your touched, filled my soul with joy.

What can I do, but suffer:

- Through my thoughts.
- Through my feelings.
- And, accept how much I love you.

To not love you, would cause me:

- Painful thoughts.
- Painful feelings.
- The same pain, as losing you to another person.

May you know this day and, every day of our lives together. How much I love you.

And how much, you have touched my life.

What Can I Say!

What can I say?

- To calm your thoughts.
- To ease your heart.
- To let you know, my words are real.
- To let you know, my thoughts are true.
- To let you know, my actions are honest.

What can we do?

But open our hearts to each other and, allow God to bless our love. I have said all I need to say!

To say any more, may create doubtful thoughts. To say any less, may cause your heart to reject my love.

So my love, I wait on your heart and soul to love me.

I want you to know my words are true, not only today but always. My words are spoken from my heart and soul.

That wants to be with you until the end of our lives together.

I've Been Waiting for You

When our journey causes us to not be together, I want you to know.
"I'll be waiting for you!"

You may have to travel, a great distance to get home. But I'll be waiting for you!

You may encounter many obstacles and, detours in your journey home.

But I'll be waiting for you!

You may get home weak and, worn from work and your journey. But I'll be waiting for you!

When you arrive home and, put away your things. I am happy, you made it home safely.

I thank God and, give you a hug and a kiss, to let you know how happy I am to see you.

I always want you to know, how much I love you. And, I'll stop waiting on you!

You Already Know!

You already know how much I love you. I say it to help remove any doubts.

You already know:

How much I enjoy being by your side.

By standing beside you and, not ahead of you. How happy I am you're in my life.

By loving you, every moment we're together.

Your love has filled my heart with joy. I let you know by doing everything in my power to make you happy. If I had just a few of this world's richest. I would buy you the desires of your heart. With all the obstacles in our path over the years. God blessed our paths to touch. God knows everything, we have done for him and our families. Because of our labors, faith and love for God. He's blessing us to enjoy the rewards of his grace, mercy and love.

By asking God to forgive us, for our mistakes and sins. God has blesses us to enjoy the beautiful life he has for us. For all the times we were lonely, God saw our tears and heard our pain. Because we didn't allow our understanding, pride and sins to block God's wisdom and love for our lives. God's love will blessed us to be together until the end of our lives together. As we travel together, down God's highway toward heaven.

I am happy for all the years God has given us to be together. I look forward to enjoying the years ahead. We're grateful for all the years, God will bless us with in the future.

Happy Birthday!

The kindness of your heart, can't be expressed by my words. My words can't describe what you have done for me, your family and friends. I am writing these few words to wish you a happy birthday.

And to let you know how much I love you!

I am writing to thank you for sharing your heart, soul and God's spirit of love with me. You and, the Holy Spirit have brought me back from the darkness of grief, loneliness and anger. I am writing to let you know your family, friends and I. Love you very much. Unknowingly, your actions of love has brightened our path. We realize the light from your soul, is only matched by the spirit of Gods' angel. We rejoice with you on your birthday and, want the best for you today and always.

Be strong on your journey, the challenges of life will try to weaken your mind, body and soul. The challenges of this world will only last for a little while. Our rewards of joy comes from our enduring our little while.

When your birthday passes don't let:

- People who are trapped and, imprisoned by this world weaken you.
- Anyone block your path, or stop your joyful spirit of love.
- People lost in darkness, block God's light of love, from your heart and soul.

Let your faith in God lift you above, the people and things in life which seek to harm you. When you become weak allow God's grace and, the memories of your loved ones to give you strength. God has called them home but, let their sacrifices of love and faith help you on you journey.

Allow their memories:

- Of hope and, faith to be added to yours.
- To renew your peace and, joy of life.
- To renew you faith, in God's Holy Spirit.

Allow God's love and, their memories to give you hope and faith.

For the storms which will touch your life.

Happy Birthday my love!

I wish you, many more in your future!

To My Wife

To my friend!
To my spiritual sister! To my soul mate!

I am writing these Valentine thoughts from my heart to yours. They're written to let you know, all the things you have become in my life.

My thoughts of love for you:

- Extend beyond the meaning of today.
- Are a reflection of our future and, life together.
- Bonds our relationship in faith and love.

My love for you will remain, long after this day has passed away. The communication, understanding and respect we've achieved. Has rewarded us with love and a life together.

May you know this day and, every day we're together how much I truly love you.

The happiness you have brought into my life, can't be measured by the things of this world.

Happy Valentine Day! My beloved wife!

I Love you now and forever!

Happy Birthday! "Tina"

Once again God has blessed you, to celebrate another birthday. During your celebration God shows you his love and the love of your parents and loved ones.

Once again God has:

- Touched your life with another year.
- Restored his love and, mercies in your life.
- Blessed us, to share another year together.

When you celebrate your birthday, you're celebrating the love of God, your parents and love ones. Your birthday celebrates years of love, which God and your parents have given you. Your birthday acknowledges the sacrifices of parents who are with God. Don't allow anyone, or anything to take away one second of joy from this day.

Or any day, God blesses you to see!

Every minute of this day is purchased with:

- The sacrifices of love, from your family and loved ones.
- God's mercies, grace and love.
- The blood of God's son, Jesus.

You my Love have purchased this day with your hard work and, your faith in God.

Therefore my beloved wife, enjoy every second of your birthday. Because it's a gift of love from God to you. We thank God, for his purchase. And ask him to be with you and, comfort you in the future.

Ok, you can tell me! How old are you again 50?

As my cousin Robert Jr. once told me, "There's no more of the 40, 40, 40 stuff!"

You're 50 now baby!

From you loving husband, Waldo!

If It Wasn't for You!

I am taking this opportunity to tell you. That loving you has brighten my life. God and, my love for you has compelled me to tell you.

How much I love you and, need you in my life.
You have unselfishly:

- Brought joy, happiness and, love into my life.
- Shared your life and, love with me.
- Helped my faith and, love for God grow.

Your heart has helped, restored my faith in my dreams and goals. Your love, has helped me enjoy the true joys of life. The kindness of your soul, has given me a soulmate for life. Without doubt or regret, I can truly say if it hadn't been for you.

I wouldn't want to:

- Suffer the challenges and, pains of this life.
- Achieve my dreams or goals.
- Surrender my will or life to God.

My heart would have die of pain and, loneliness without you in my life.

Because of you:

- I endure the challenges of life.
- My dreams and, goals are renewed and alive.
- My faith in God has given me joy, happiness and love.

Because of your loving heart and, spirit my soul wants to share eternity with you. As we journey toward a known and unknown future together. I am happy you're in my life.

I am happy to know, whatever lies ahead for us.

God will bless us, to face it together as one heart, spirit and soul.

A House from God

T his letter was written to my loving wife Tina. For all the gift's she didn't receive in life. After finding a problem on my credit report, which prevented us from purchasing our first home. My heart was filled with pain, knowing my past actions blocked our path to a home together. It hurts to know we must wait, to enjoy the simple pleasures of a home together. With all the challenges in life, we have already endured. We have to wait for God to bless our request.

Waiting is like a:

- A slow death.
- An unseen and, untouched joy.
- A prolonged pain, forcing us forward without a destination.

For a little while longer, we must wait in faith and patience on our options. We have to wait and allow God and, our efforts time to remove the obstacles in our path. We won't allow this challenge to steal our joy or block the joy of a home. While we wait, we will continue to grow in determination, courage, love and faith. Our faith and love in God has already purchased the home we need. Our courage and, determination has planted the seeds of belief for

God to bless. Our love for each other, has replaced the homes we didn't receive. Our spirit of love for each other, and our faith in God want let us stop or give up.

Four months, after writing this spiritual letter. God blessed us with a beautiful home. The home God blessed us, with had over a year worth of equality after the purchase. Two weeks after moving into our home, Tina was laid-off. After working nineteen years, with the same company. Tina's unselfish efforts, to help me with my debits. Allowed me to pay the mortgage with one check. God not only blessed us, with the home of our dreams. Because we thanked him and, not our efforts. God made sure we could afford and keep it!

Thank you God!

For the earthly treasures you allowed us to enjoy on this side, for a little while!

We Don't Have to Like It! But, We Have to Get Through It!

I made this statement, in response to a conflict Tina had with a new supervisor. Because of his insecurities, the supervisor enjoyed micro-managed his employees. The poor work habits of younger employees, created stricter working standards for everyone in her department. Unlike the younger employees in her department, Tina performs her job responsibilities as required without supervision. Tina and her co-worker were upset, at the strict working rules caused by younger co-workers. The same working standards may happen to us and, many other workers in the job market. When doing our best isn't good enough:

- Because other workers create work problems, which affect us.
- We have to get through it!
- When our opinions could help an important decision.

But we're not allowed to give our option. We have to get through it! When co-workers, or a supervisor make decisions. Then blame us for their mistakes. We defiantly don't have to like it! These problems exist in life challenges and, the storms of life. We can't allow our emotions, or other people to stop us. From during our best for our future and, our families. Don't carry around the bad decisions, problems, mistakes, hatred, guilt or shame of others. We don't have to like the person, place, emotion or things.

But, we have to get through it! Let it go!

Anything that controls our thoughts, emotions and actions is our master. Whatever we allow to upsets us, or make us angry controls us! Anything or anyone which is harmfully affect us in any form, has to be identified, checked and resolved.

Therefore beloved, unless we:

- Know what the problem is, we don't know how to fight it!
- Give it strength it's weak.
- Feed it, it'll die.

We can't allow our thoughts, emotions or pride to take us into darkness. We should only look back at darkness, to learn for it.

Don't allow:

- Past mistakes, situations, or events define who you are.
- Anyone tell us, we're not worthy of God's blessing or love.

Remember the words and, actions of our parents and loved ones.

Learn from their actions, mistakes and faith. God and, our loved ones help us realize:

- If we're weak, we have chosen to be weak.
- If any of us are confused about God's grace and, mercies in our life. It's because we have rejected it and have chosen to be confused.
- If any of us don't know the path to heaven.

It's because we have rejected our faith in God and, what our parents and loved ones taught us.

By writing this letter to you, it reminds me of the times you helped me. When things got difficult you reminded me of God's blessing and, what he has already brought us through. When we didn't have enough money to pay all our bills. You reminded me of a time when we didn't have a job or money for bills. When we look at our life, we're learn to be grateful to God for what he has given us. We're grateful for where we are and, who's we are! Regardless of the difficulties in life, we must always learn to be grateful. Because there are people with bigger crosses to bear in life. Who wish they had our problems!

Therefore, if we fail let us fail:

• Doing our will and, purpose in our life.
• In our pride, selfishness, wants and desires.
• Doing God will and, purpose in our life.

If we don't succeed to our standards or, the standards of our family and God's world.

Let us truthfully say, "I did my best!" Take joy in knowing we did our best!

That's all God and, our parents ask us to do!

To My Son

To My Son

To my son Reginald, the last "Theus" from my family. To carry our family name into the future. May the joy, happiness and love of God, be with you and, your wife Tennessa. I hope and, pray when my life on this side ends. I have stored up a few earthly treasures, to help you and your family on your journey.

But, until that day comes!

The only earthly treasures I have to give you, are the experiences of my life.

And a small amount of wisdom, which God blessed me to acquire and keep.

In my spiritual letters written to you and, your family. I leave you these things in my book(s).

I pray they continue to give you and, your family strength, courage and faith on your journey and in your life.

Words to Love By!

I pray this spiritual letter blesses you and, your family to grow in faith and love. Your communication, understanding, respect for each other. Your faith in God, are the building blocks of your lives together. Your communication will bring understanding, so talk with Tennessa about everything. Talk about small and, large problems which affect you her and your family. The understanding which you'll acquire from your communication, will place a protected wall of respect around your lives and love.

Your walls of respect will keep your thoughts, emotions, mistakes and love safe. For each other and, away from people that seek to control or destroy your family and love. Your walls of respect will help you, cherish the love you have in your hearts for each other. Your love is a protected roof over you lives, and your family. Which will shield you from storms caused by people, problems and life. Don't let the storms created by your differences or the people outside your home tear you and your family apart.

Continue to strengthen your mind, body and spirit daily in preparation for storms. You can't allow any of them to become weak, damaged or injured.

Treasure what God has given you:

- Don't allow anything or anyone, to bring harm or pain to you or your family.
- Don't allow anyone, or anything to turn you away from God or each other.
- Always thank God, for his blessing and love.

If you do these things and, you can! God will fill your life with peace and joy! When you journey on his side has ended. Your greatest happiness is knowing you both did your best, to make each other and your family happy.

My greatest reward, is knowing I did my best. To help you, in your journey.

Take care of each other and, your families. I love you both!

Congratulations to My Son

This letter was written to my son, a few weeks after his promotion to Regional Director of his company.

Words can't express how happy and, proud I am of you. And how much I want the best for you and, your family. When I spoke to you about your promotion.

My words were said to:

- Encourage you, but they caused you anxiety.
- Help prevent future mistakes, but they made your upset.
- Guide you in future decisions but, they made you remember the pain of your past mistakes.

My statements were said, to help you focus on your family. But you helped me realize, you were taught that as a child. My words were spoken, from a heart filled with pride and love. Therefore my beloved son, use those words which help you and your family.

If anything I said, blocks your path:

- Remove it, from your thoughts.
- Go around those, which slow you down.
- Cut though those, which threaten your peace.
- Rise above those, which make you upset or cause you to become anger.

Ignore everything and, everyone which doesn't help you, or your family in life. For all the things, I wanted to give you. My advice is the only treasure I have left. I hope you can learn from my mistakes! When my mistakes prevented me from being by your side. My mind never stopped thinking about you and, my heart and soul never stop loving you.

Our love for God, our self and, our loved ones must be first in our Life.

God and, your loves ones will journey with you until you reach heaven.

Desires and Consequences

I wrote this spiritual letter in the fall of 2011, for my son and me. It's a reminder of my life alone, even with people all around me. God was the only one with me in a life, which exist in my memories.

By allowing my pride, selfness and stubbornness, to set my selfish wants and desires free to control my life.

The consequences of my decisions and, actions were the cost I paid for their freedom. I thought about my consequences last week, after talking to you. While talking to my son, the memories of his childhood touched my heart and soul. The only toy he went to sleep with, was a ceramic bass guitar. Which played, Beethoven's 5th symphony. "Even as a baby, he begin developing the mind of a genius."

I left my son because of:

- My words, actions and consequences.
- My selfishness, pride and stubbornness.
- My desires for the earthly treasures of God's world.

My love for God and, my son helped me endured my actions and, consequences of actions.

Because of my selfish decisions in life:

- My educational achievements, were unaccomplished.
- My financial worth, was never achieved.
- The earthly treasures I valued, were lost, stolen or sold.

Because of my lack of faith in God, his Holy Spirit. It became trapped inside a temple of pride, stubbornness and sin. As the years passed, my young body has become a victim of age. The wonderful mind, which God gave me to help others. Was wasted on selfish wants and desires. My heart and, soul rejected God out of respect and fear. I was stubborn and filled with pride! But I wasn't going to do anything to disrespect God. When God stopped me on my journey, I found myself alone and in darkness. The pain, anger and grief of our mother's death, was touching my heart. The death of my mother, helped me return to God's holy light. By surrendering to God's will and purpose for my life. The Holy Spirit blessed me, to see the beauty of my life. I realized the treasures in my body and health. The mind which God gave me, to help others was now used to counsel my family members, loved ones and friends.

After paying the cost for my consequences:

- I enjoy, the beauty of life.
- I smile, at my past and the future.
- I journey, toward God and heaven in joy.

I am writing this letter, to everyone that has to live with life consequences. My love for God, helped me return to his holy light. Let my words touch your heart and soul. When time becomes my enemy and, my son's friend. I am happy to know he was raised to love God, his wife and family.

After writing this spiritual letter, a memory about my sister

Stephanie made me smile. When I returned home from Dallas, my sister Stephanie would always say, Amen!

With a smile she would say, "Our brother, the prodigal son"! Has returned home from the wildness and, a life of sinful living." What she didn't know was her brother was changing with each visit I made home.

Her brother started to realize, he was returning home:

- To his family, that truly loved him.
- With the earthly treasure, of his family love in his heart.
- With the humble spirit of a servant.

Rather than returning home with the heart of the master. I was returned home with the spirit and, soul of a servant. Most of all, I was returning home having accepted God's will and, love in my life.

Blessed are those that find God on this side!

Before they stand, before the "Trinity" on the other side! What I said to you as a child, I now say to you as a man.

"Continue to ask God to heal you and, your family spiritually, emotionally and physically."

You father, Waldo!

The New Generation

T he new generation, was written a few months after the birth of my first granddaughter, Jordyn D Theus. She was born in August 2011, at 4:55 am.

A new joy of life, arrives with each new generation. They arrive as weak babies, unaware of the people and, world around them. They're the children of our children and, the babies of our future. They're the future parents and, generations of God's world. With help from God and, their parents the new generation will grow, into strong men and women. As older family members end their journey on this side. It's the new generation, which will replace them and us. When time attacks our thoughts and body, the new generation will become stronger and wiser. God's love and, his time clock of life is counting down our years and, those of our new generation.

When our knowledge of this world fades away, the new generation will grow in understanding and wisdom. When God calls his Holy Spirit and, our soul to rest in heaven. Our light will become dim until it disappears. But the light of life for our new generation, will grow as bright as the sun. We rejoice in their present and life, as our journey reaches its end.

With love in our heart we teach them and, their parents everything we know. Only to have our knowledge used against us.

We give the new generation and, their parents:

- All we have, only to be told it's not enough.
- Our experiences, wisdom and dreams.
- Only to be told they know what they need and want.
- Our understanding and, faith in God's love.

Only to be told, they didn't ask to be here! We teach them they can't have everything they want. We continue to look into the faces of our generation and, their parents with love in our heart. We ask our self? What more can we do, or say to help prepare them for their journey in life. They ask us for help, then thank us by asking, "Is this all you have to give me" With joy and, pain in our hearts we say, "Yes it's all I have if you used it wisely, it's all you need!"

We remind them to cherish life and, look up to God for help. Rather than looking around to the people and, temporary things of God's world. We tell them, that God's time clock of life, makes each day of life precious. We tell them to live, plan and save for their future, while they're young. We remind them to not let mistakes, failures and problems, stop them from enjoying life.

After saying and, doing everything we can to help them. We're happy to know we did our best! We have made the sacrifices of love, needed to help them. And, their parents prepare for their journey. We'll rest in peace knowing we did everything we could to help them in their journey. We pray to God to bless our children and, future generation. The new generation and, their parents no longer wants to hear our words. We have to learn to let our belief and, faith in God replace our words. The knowledge and, faith we shared with them want be forgotten. Even if they think, they know everything!

Before our life on this side comes to an end, we tell them that we love them. We remind them to control their emotions and, choose their friends carefully. We tell them, to choose their own path in life. Because if we continue to giving them advice, many of them will go the other direction out of pride and stubbornness. With the love of God in our spirit, we remind them to take care of them self and, their families. When they get older their faith will help them realizing God, we'll be waiting on their arrival in heaven.

Before we leave this side, we never stop encouraging our children.

Because one day they will choose, to journey toward God and us.

Or, in the other direction!

To Marti

Marti Croft

M arti Croft was the Assistant Vice-President of Corporate Service for my company. I was a building engineer, which made Marti my direct supervisor. Our friendship developed from us working together. Marti's spirit was similar to my mother's.

Marti passed away December 2009, five months after my mother. Another type of cancer, ended her life on this side years too early. During the last five months of her life, I wrote Marti a number of emails. A couple of my e-mails, were written months after her death.

Because of her spirit and, our friendship Marti earned a place in my heart. And in this book, which honors the life of my mother.

I'm Praying for You!

I am happy to hear you're doing better and, in good spirits. I know you're returning from what feels like a bottomless pit.

My prayers are with you and, our mother daily. She's about to enter, the same bottomless pit you experienced. Unfortunately, her pit will be deeper and, filled with more challenges when she returns. A 5:00 pm phone call from my sister, Stephanie. Tuesday night informed me of our mother's third visit, to the emergency room in two weeks. During his visit, a large mass was found on one of her kidneys. Additional tests, reviled one of her kidneys was abnormal from childhood. A small hole was found in her right hip, from a fall she suffered years ago.

My family and, I are praying her biopsy is negative. We found out she will have to live without one of her kidneys. Which will require her to have weekly dialysis treatments, to live a normal life. The operation to remove her kidney is still in the planning stage pending additional tests.

It's during times of illness and, death we realize the beauty of the life, which God has given us. The challenges of living gives us hope and, faith in God to help us endure life. One of our main joy in life is the love of our family and knowing, we did our best!

When our life ends, God and we may be the only ones that knows it was our best!

When the light of hope increases your sight and, awareness returns to your mind. I want you to know how much we miss and love you. You already know, "You can't do anything about it!

There are employees:

- That care about you but, they will never say a word to let you know how they feel.
- That admire your strength and, knowledge but they will chal- lenge every decision you make.
- That wanted to tell you the truth, but their laziness has silenced their words.

Other employees work hard, to make you proud. But their insecurities has filled them with proud and, selfish. Lastly, you have employees that think too much. Which prevents them from showing and, telling you how much they truly care for you.

From me and, all your employees take care of yourself. We look forward to you returning to work!

Thinking of You!

I wrote this letter to Marti in Nov 2009, a few weeks before she passed away. Because of her illness, she didn't have an opportunity to read it.

These are just a few words to let you know, I and many others in the department and, company are thinking about you. I know you're going through a difficult time with your cancer treatments.

But don't give up!

Continue to stay strong and fight, do whatever it takes to make yourself better. Endure whatever needs to be endured to get well. My mother didn't have an opportunity to fight her cancer. When we go through challenges God and, our loved ones are there to help us.

They teach us:

- To endure the difficulties and, pains of life.
- To persevere with hope and, faith in God.
- With God's help, we can endure any challenge.

By remembering what our parents and, loved one taught us will keep us from give up! The love of your co-worker is fighting with you. I told our mother to continue fighting "Just for a little while". With God's help we only have to endure the pains and, challenges of life, just for a little while anyway.

I pray that God allows, your little while to be short! Your difficulties and, pains to be few!

Journey home in peace and, love my friend! You will be truly missed, on this side!

A Final Goodbye

To Marti,
   Thank you for the:

- Opportunity, to work with you.
- Promises, I was allowed to keep.
- Songs and, events we shared together.

Thank you, for the times you helped me at work and in life. I submit daily prayers to God for you and our mother.

I pray that God's love touches:

- Your thoughts.
- Your body
- Your soul.

I pray that God's mercy, grace and love continues to comforts you on your journey.

Back to him and, your loved ones in heaven. You are truly missed!

What Would She Say?

This spiritual letter was written because of departmental conflicts.

Which occurred a year after Marti death. It was written to remind me and, other employee's. What Marti would have said about our words and actions. I challenged my co-workers to look at our words and actions. Then compare them to the standards set by Marti.

Marti would have been:

- Proud, but disappointed.
- She would have been proud of our work but, disappointed in our words.
- Angry, but smiled anyway. She would have smiled at our effort. But angry about our behavior and, how we treated each other.

She would have written us up but, given us a second chance to correct our actions. Marti would have been sad, but happy. She would have been sad, we haven't learned from her examples and teachings. But she's happy, knowing she did her best to help each of us. Marti would have told us, we're acting like children again! Knowing our individual problems, she would have told us just what she thought about our actions. Then she would have challenged us to be better. She would smile to let each of us know she hasn't given up on us.

Let us not dishonor Marti's memory, by giving up on each other. Or by making the same mistakes, over and over again. While working together, I remember telling Marti many times. "It's a different mistake!" She would look at me and, smile while shaking her head.

While journeying toward Marti:

- Our words and, actions should honor her memory.
- Let us not be deceived, by pride or what we feel.

The temporary emotions we feel, will pass away if we're truly upset at Marti's loss.

We honor her by being:

- Understanding.
- Strong and determined.
- Our best, as she was.

In her our way Marti let each of us know, how much she truly cared for us. When we look at our self and, each other's words and actions.

They should let Marti know how much we cared for her!

There's Nothing Left to Say!

After my spiritual letter, "What Would She Say!" didn't help my co-workers. I wrote this spiritual letter to help me, deal with their words and actions. When I look back at my decisions, relationships, marriages, jobs and life. I look forward, to a life with faith in God.

There's nothing left to say about the:

- Words I spoke, or the actions I performed.
- Ideas and, effort I have shown.
- Years of sacrifices and, unending hours of work.
- Broken promises and, forgotten lies.

For all the promotions, bonuses and raises I didn't received. There's nothing left to say! For all the meaningless compliments and, thoughtless thank you. There's nothing left to say! With God's help, I allow my faith and, determination to help me endure your promises and lies. They're like dreams, which will fade away.

I will continue to work, at the highest level my training and educa- tion allows. I gladly sacrifice my wants and, allow my needs to make my life happy. Regardless of my title, or pay. I want let you or anyone, keep me from doing my best or being my best.

Unlike those that:

- Live in hopelessness and, darkness.
- Rejoice in lies and, deceit.
- Fear being wrong.

I renew my spirit and, soul daily in truth and faith. Unlike those that rejoice in lying, over and over again and still make the same mistakes. I choose to learn from my mistakes and, not make them again. People that enjoy their position but, not the responsibility of their position. Never learn to do their best or be there best in life!

When you read my words, hid them:

- In your mind.
- In your heart.
- In your soul.

Allow them to help you, with the people of his world which cause trouble in your life. Because the God we serve sees all, hears all and judges all! Knowing the things of his world are temporary. Those in darkness can't see the light of God in their life. They're troubled by every event, which occurs in their life. They're preparing for an entirety life, without God unless they change. Those in God's holy light, enjoy all the peace and joys life offers. They allow the blessing of God's Holy Spirit to touch their soul and life.

When we allow the Holy Spirit into our life, we become the beautiful angel God created!

Stop complaining about the people and, things in God's world that we can't change.

We have to focus on becoming the beautiful angel, which God created us to be!

To My Family and Friends

Waiting on Love!

I wrote this spiritual letter in June 2011, to a coworker who was waiting on love. During one of your relationships, a man desiring to been your soul mate waited on you. He left because you didn't see him, or you were in another relationship. One day God will allow him, or someone even better to come into your life. Before God blesses another man to come into your life. Your mind will question God's will, purpose and wisdom.

You will ask God:

- How long will it be?
- Who will it be?
- What will he look like?
- Will he be older or younger than me?

Your faith and, patience in God will answer your first question. You know from your past relationships, it's better to be along in peace. Than be with someone that brings unhappiness and pain into your life. Who will it be?

It may not be, the man directly in front of you. But he knows you and, has always been close to you. You will look around wondering. What will he look like? You know from past relationships, that everything that looked good wasn't good for you. His features maybe plain, but look at the beauty of his heart and soul.

Will he be older, or younger than me?

Regardless of his age, look at his heart and soul. Our journey through life isn't happy, when we travel lone. Allow your faith and, patience in God to tell you when it's time. God may require you to wait three, or four times longer than your last relationship. Your waiting period will allow your heart and, soul time to heal. From the relationships which didn't endure conflicts and problems.

During your healing process allow:

- The pains, of your past relationships be removed.
- Your thoughts, to think about good times and things ahead.
- The Holy Spirit to open your heart, to the joys of love and life.

Most of all let your faith and, love in God bind the desires of your thoughts. Which, caused you to turn away from God's love. When you do these things, and you can!

God will send you a soul mate to spend eternity with you on this side.

Take care of yourself, your loved ones and family. Your friend, Waldo

A Day of Love

Each day of life reminds us of our love for God, our parents and loved ones. When challenges, fear and pains try to destroy our joy for life.

We allow our:

- Belief in God, to strengthen our soul.
- Hope, to fill our thoughts and heart with happiness.
- Faith in the Holy Spirit, to guide and comfort us in joy.

When we allow God's blessings of love, to touch us. He'll be in our life forever! Don't let our words say, "I love you!" and our actions make us a liar! If we allow this to occur, we are deceiving God and our self.

Our actions should show:

- Our true feeling of love.
- A sincere heart of hope.
- The purity of our faith, love and soul.

Our actions should shows God, and our loved ones a love from our soul. They proved their love for us, through their words and actions. During our sacrifices of love, we prove our love daily by our words and actions. When we love God and, do his will it moves us close to his holiness.

Regardless of what we have done, doing or going through in life. God's love and, our parent's memories will sustain us until we're on the other side with them!

So make each day, one of love!

Your Hearts

Your heart was written August 2012 for Carrie, Tamera, Darlene and Pam. A few of Tina's and, my closest friends.

We realize your hearts, has the spirit of an angel. We cherish and enjoy every minute we're in your presence. Your faith in God helps us realize, we want always get or receive what we deserve on this side. Your life makes us thankful for the time God has blessed us to be together on this side.

The pains, trails, grief and challenges in God's world. Helps prepare us for a new life on the other side. We know the troubles of life, will only last for a little while as God prepares us for heaven. We know our life, on this side must end one day. The temporary friendship we share on this side, is replaced with an eternity friendship in heaven. When we pass away from his world, we know it's God's way of returning us home. We will cry tears of pain and, joy for each other until we're united in heaven.

Whenever there is love for someone on this side. Pain and grief are there forcing our faith, to ask God to help us. Enduring pain is difficult, but we know with God's help "It'll only last for a little while!"

During our little while:

- Our pains and, challenges of life grow our hope.
- Our love for God, strengthen our belief and faith.
- We allow God's Holy Spirit to love us through our pains and his world.

During our "little while," we know God will comforts us until we're together again.

Take care of yourself dear friends, until we're united in heaven!

Happy Birthday, Arletta!

Written to Arletta, July 2012.
I am writing to wish you a happy birthday!

The "Birthday's" behind you are many. I pray that God continues to bless you with many more "Birthday's" in your future.

Your hair is grayer! But, God has renews your spirit and, soul daily.

Your body has aged, but God has blesses everything, to keep working.

Your pace is slower, but when God has directed your path from childhood.

When we journey toward God and, our loved ones.

Take joy in knowing, only God knows when you will arrive home. Until then, allow him to bless you with "Birthday's" of joy.

You friend always, Waldo!

Mistakes and Consequences

Why me? What did I do?

From the beginning of our lives, we learned to endure our human limitations. When we took our first steps, we were unknowingly starting our journey toward God. During our first steps, we would sometime fell and injure our self. The pains and, scares were the price we paid for our independence and freedom. When we begin to talk, thousands of words would enter our thoughts. Many of our words were wrong or come out backward. Our mistakes would cause family members and, loved ones to laugh at us.

"I am talking about you, my beloved Stephanie!"

After we grew into adults our parents and, the world teaches us about life. And what we need to do to take care of our self. Before starting our journey in life, we have so much to learn. Our knowledge, life and the world around us. Forces us to ask our self, 'How will I make it? Then many of us would turn around and, ask God why me? Our first mistake is taking God's power away from him. By asking, "How will I make it? Then we have the nerve to blame God for the problems we created in our life. God made us in his image but, made us subject to human weaknesses, mistakes and consequences.

What did I do? Nothing!

God has blessed us to be born from the love of Jesus, his Holy Spirit and our parents. When we live and, enjoy the life they have given us. We continually fight with them for our freedom and independent. Instead of loving God and our parents, we turn away from them. We let our actions, mistakes, knowledge become our teachers. Our thoughts, pride and actions blocks our path to the "Trinity" and heaven.

The gift of life from God, answers our "Why me question?" Along with the blessing of Jesus, God has given us one of the most precious treasure he has, "Life." Our physical bodies, mind and soul are a spiritual blessing from God. God has blessed us with them so we can enjoy our life on this side.

Our faith in God's:

- Word, helps strengthen us in belief and hope.
- Mercy and, grace helps us accept our mistakes and consequences.
- Love, will heal us from our sins through his grace and mercy.

You still want to ask, What did I do? Our words and, actions are a living record of our life. They're recorded in Gods' "Book of life". Knowing this we have nothing to fear, lie about or be ashamed of. We're the only ones blocking our path, to God and heaven. Our faith in God's love is our key, which opens the doors between us and the other side. God has given us "A little while" to enjoy the beauty of life and use our key of faith. God's love, peace and joy will be with us always. "If we surrender our life to his will and purpose!" We should starting asking our self these questions.

Why want I surrender my life to God and, let him help me? What's stopping me? Do you think, it makes us look weak?

When we can truthfully answer these questions.

We know who and, what keeps us a prisoner in life!"

Our Hearts

I wrote this spiritual letter, after the two years anniversary of our mother death. The memory of her love and, life brought tears to my eyes. Pain filled thoughts, heart and soul.

God has given us a wonderful heart, as a gift of love and life. About the size of a grapefruit, our heart sustains a body hundreds of times its size. It provides every part of our body with nourishment it needs to function, grow and survive. It provides our brain with the nutriments to think and, the power to control every movement of our body.

With all the knowledge and, abilities the brain has. It would be useless without the heart to sustain it. After reading all the books, which have been written. And taken all the classes, which have been taught. With all the knowledge mankind has learned about the brain and heart, he has no power to control them. We are like a child, looking through God's window of knowledge. We desires to control God's knowledge. But, we realizes we can only master a cup fill of which is an enormous ocean. The heart and, brain function together to supply our body with what it needs to live and survive. They're not the masters of the body, they're servants to the needs of the body. They help the body think, reason move and function as God has designed it.

The same is true of mankind, we're servants to the needs of God and our life. God, Jesus and the Holy Spirit are the spiritual substances. Which nourish us to function and live. We would have never existed, if it wasn't God's will and purpose. If we wanted it or not! Like it or not! We're born as blessing to God's mercy, power and love. Because of his love for us, he gave us his son Jesus, and his Holy Spirit. God gives use his Holy Spirit to comfort, teach and guide us toward his holiness. When we awaken from our sleep of death, we're grateful for each day God blesses us to see. Before we enjoy the desires of our heart, we should remember God's heart is in our body. When our thoughts focuses on our lustful wants, rather than our spiritual needs. We should remember God's needs, for our life should be our first thought. When we lift our self up in pride, remember the Holy Spirit lives in the temple of our body. Even when our days reach their end, we should never think you're alone. The same God that created us in the beginning of our life. Will be with us until the end of our life. If we allow him to be there!

Like our heart, God has provided all our needs in life. If we feel alone, it's because we're doing our will and, not the will of God. It's during these times in our life, we want to be the master. Rather than the humble servant, which surrenders himself to God's mercy, grace and love. Like a disobedient children, returning to a loving parents. We must return to the God that created and loves us. Upon our return, outside the gates of heaven.

A loving God looks into his, "Book of life".

With a tear of grace in his eyes, as we stand before Jesus and his Holy Spirit. God turns millions and millions of pages. From a short distance away, we see Jesus sacrificed blood covering every page. Before God reaches our name we see Jesus smiling at us. We feel God's Holy Spirit hugging us with Love! After God reaches our name he looks up. With a tear of mercy falling from his eye toward our name.

God looks at us and says, "Here you are my child!" When tears of love leave his eyes and, fall toward the page. Because you praised me, repented your sins, and accepted my son Jesus as your savior. And allowed my Holy Spirit, to dwell in the temple of your soul. Everything you thought, said and did in your life has been forgiven. By my by our mercy, grace and love. The blood of my son Jesus and, my Holy Spirit has prepared you with holiness to enter my holy temple."

After God finished speaking, "The doors of hell closed and, the gates of heaven opens, to our loved ones"

Let your faith and, the love for God touch your heart, mind and soul.

Every day of your life on this side!

Simple Pleasures

T his is one of seven letters written to my family and, loved ones the first year after our mother passed away. Four of the seven letters has the word, "Life" in the title. Each letter is written to celebrate God's love for us.

Because of our carnal mind and life on this side, God continues to bless us. As time passes, we feel our life losing its flavor and taste. Joy leaves our life when we lose the simple pleasures in life, which made us happy. We're only left with the sweet memories of our loved ones. Which are no longer in our life. The sweet memories and, simple pleasures we shared with them. Helped us endure the challenges of life and enjoy simple pleasures, like eating and drinking during the holiday seasons.

The smell of cooked chicken, reminds me of the chicken my mother cooked when was with us. These foods and, many others have become a part of my past and memories in life. When I think about my favorite meal, fried chicken, spaghetti, greens, macaroni and cheese and cornbread. These are a few of the many foods, which will never look or taste the same. Without my loved ones here to cook them.

Why you ask?

Our loved ones used different seasoning and ingredients. Which gave food a different smell and taste. They added a labor of love to their cooking which can't be duplicate. The food of today doesn't look or taste the same as the food of my past. It has the nutritional value to nourish my body. But, it has lost its taste and pleasure in my life. The wonder smells and, taste of food prepared by my loved ones will never leave my memories. Their memories of their loss, forces us me return to a life of simple living and pleasures.

Their love and memories are timeless pieces of my heart and soul. Without them with me the pleasure of this life has a bitter taste. God doesn't allows us to see, touched or hear our loved ones on this side. But his Holy Spirit blesses us to feel the essence of their life in our soul. Because their essence is still with us. We're forced to enjoy the simple pleasures of life with a bitter taste of happiness and joy. The sweet memories of our love ones lives. Leaves behind an aroma of love to what would be a painful life.

When we allows their loving memories to season our life:

- We're able to endure the pains and, challenges of life.
- Their love give us courage, to face our fears, mistakes and consequences.
- We allow our faith in God, to guide our life.

During our simple pleasure of peace, the Holy Spirit blesses us to remember their echoes of love from heaven.

Their echoes of love tells us God's world is:

- A pit stop, on our way to heaven!
- A short walk, down a dark alley.
- The last thing we'll see, before the light of heaven is reviled.

While traveling toward our final destination, we realize our journey on this side is short. We learn to enjoy our loved on this side and, the simple pleasures our life has to offer. Our faith in God, helps us prepare for the sweet pleasures of heaven. Which can't be seen, or felt from this side.

Until we cross-over to the other side, the biggest family reunion hasn't occurred. Our loved ones final words haven't been heard, their loving embrace hasn't been felt. Their sweetest cakes and, pies haven't been baked or tasted. They're waiting on our arrival, with open arms. When our simple pleasures in life and, God's world are ending.

We're preparing and, ready:

- To leave, for the other side.
- To join, our family reunion.
- To taste the sweet cake and, pies made by God and our loved ones.

Most of all we're ready to hear the welcome words of God, and embrace our loved ones on the other side.

Don't let the earthly pleasures and, desires of this life.

Keep you from an eternal life with God and, our loved ones in heaven!

Life's Journey

L ife's journey was written in July 2011, to encourage Pastor Mc Neil during his mother illness.

God has blessed us to live and, enjoy a beautiful life. He watched over us, as we entered his world. And comforted us though our storms and, those of our loved ones. He lovely cared for us, through our sickness, pains and hopelessness. He blesses us, to enjoy the earthly treasures of our life and his world.

After all God has done for us, Why do we?

- Disobey and, fear a God that has taken care of our needs and, many of our wants.
- Think of God first but, we put him last in our life.
- Think God isn't with us.

The answer is simple it's our human flesh, which enjoys all the things of his world the wrong way. It's our carnal mind, which is only grateful when it has received what it wants. Rather then what it needs! It's our carnal heart, which loves everything but, puts our love for God last. Why you ask?

Because our soul is separated from the present and, love of God. We're too filled with pride, stubborn and shamed to accept or return to God's love. After having our way for years, we find our self alone and separated from God. We reject God's grace, mercy and love but, we continually asking him for blessing. We find our self, enjoying the icing of God's love with little or no faith. We have become lazy and, filled with pride to let our faith help us.

We shouldn't be troubled, about having to leave his world. If we're troubled, it's because we have done our will and, not God's will. Let us not be sad, for the loved ones we will leave on this side. God will care for them, as he has cared for us so many years. If we must be sad, let us be sad for not walking the path, which leads to God and heaven. God has already let us know, "Our loved ones are happy with him in heaven" and, "They don't want to return to this side!"

What should we do?

- Enjoy our time on this side, with our loved.
- Don't let anything, block our joy of life.
- Don't let people and, things of God's world make us unhappy or angry.

Don't let the challenges of life, take away your hope and, faith in God. Lastly don't let people, lost in darkness cause you to lose your path to God. We know our life on this side will end one day.

When our life on this side ends we'll:

- Leave behind our achievements, successes and failures.
- Leave behind our wants, desired, mistakes and consequences of our sins.
- Leave behind those we love and, that loves us.

Don't look down, in sadness and pains. We should look up with joy knowing that God, our parents are waiting on our arrival. They're waiting to let us know, our journey is over and, we're home. Because of God and, our love ones love for us we no longer fear death. We know Gods' angels will return his Holy Spirit and, us back to heaven. Death is a journey, we must take! It's a ticket to a better place. Only those that serve God, will reach their destination in heaven. Death is our first stop on our journey toward God. We know death prepares us, for another life in heaven!

Life

This spiritual letter was written after a sermon preached by Pastor Mc Neil. After God called his mother home, to be with him. God's love tells us and, always wants the best for us. The Holy Spirit wants us to know, God could have made our lives last for eternity. But we would forget about God and, try to make him our servant. God could have made our years, as numerous as the stars. But we would be ungrateful and, think we're God's. So God only gives us a little while on this side.

Our short life, helps us:

- Stop thinking we're the master of God's world.
- Remember his world isn't our home.
- Praise God and, be grateful to him for our life.

Our true home is with God and, our loved ones in heaven. God doesn't want us, to be sad for those he has called home to heaven. They're with him and, they don't want to return to this side! Our loved ones, "Don't want to return to his world."

"They're happy, to be with God in heaven!" So will we when our time comes!

Life's Purpose

Haven't we all asked our self, Why am I here? Why was I born? What's God's purpose for my life? Why are people and, things in God's world the way they are? Why does God allow it to occur and continue? I've asked myself, many of the same questions many times. I think I've found some answers, to my questions. The answers come from God, our parents and us. God uses our parents and, friends as spiritual vessels to teach us his word, commandants and will. The answers to our questions doesn't come from our knowledge, experiences or our understanding of God's world.

Our answers come from God's:

- Holy bible.
- His Holy Spirit.
- Our faith in him.

If we asked for it or not, whether we wanted life or not! God loves us, even after we turn away from him. God has always been, a loving parent to disobedient children that continually do, what they want with their lives.

God allows us to return to him after we:

- Repent our sins
- Ask for his forgiveness and mercy.
- Worship him in spirit and truth.

God gives us his Holy Spirit to help us return to him cleansed and holy. His Holy Spirit, helps us on our journey and in life. God left us his holy word, for us to understand and follow.

God's holy word will:

- Guide our thoughts, actions and emotions.
- Teach us how to have faith.
- Heal us through our pains and, sin in our life.
- Allows the Holy Spirit to comfort and heal our heart and soul.

Through his holy word and, the Holy Spirit, God has provided the answers to all our questions. Now it's up to us! What do we need to do?

We allow our faith in God's holy word to:

- Guide us.
- Teach us.
- Give us courage, strength, joy and peace.
- Help us do his will and, not our will.

Regardless of what sins we've committed, God will love us through them. We have to let the people and, things of his world be judged by God. That will never be our job! Even if some people thinks it's their job! We have to let God's grace, mercies and, love help us accept and endure our self and them.

Our faith in God's word and, his Holy Spirit will help guide through everything in life.

Which torments us and, blocks our path to him and our loved

ones. We're blessed to labor and, do God's will in the storms of life!

Because God will bless us to see the gates of heaven, even during our storms!

Life's Seasons

G od has blessed us to see another season in life. While preparing
for another year, we ask our self. What challenges will this
year bring? What people and, problems will I have to endure? It's
during these times our faith questions God will and, purpose for
our life. We know the approaching year will test and, challenge us
physical, emotional and spiritually. During the passing of time we
feel and, see its effects on our mind, body and life. Our birthdays
and, the anniversaries of our loved ones passing. Reminds us, that
each passing season of our life is precious.

"When I was a child, I thought as a child, I understood as a
child, I reasoned as a child. When I became a man, I put the ways
of childhood behind me." (1 Corinthians 13:11 NIV)

Being mature adults we're challenged to put away, the childish
things of our childhood. God and, our parents love pre-pares us for
life's seasons. Our path and, life experiences mark the paths we
chose on our journey. We have allowed the scares of our youth, to
be our symbols of growth, wisdom and faith. If we learned from
them or not, we realize the years behind us are gone forever! We
can't go back to our childhood, or past and change anything. The
loved ones, which started their journey with us, seasons ago have

reached their destination. Because of God's grace, mercy and love. We're blessed and grateful to go forward to another season.

We go forward in:

- Joy and, pain.
- Regret and, hope.
- Sadness and, happiness.
- Hopelessness and, in faith.

Because of our love for God and, our loved we don't fear the seasons ahead. We allow God to free our thoughts, heart and soul from anger. We don't allow our emotions and, actions to distract us from our journey in life. When we allow our faith and, love of God to master our fears, anger and emotions. We're close to the end of our journey, by accepting the challenges, mistakes and storms of life seasons.

We have accepted, what we need from life seasons:

- We have kept the faith and, did our best!
- We've accepted, the loss of our loved with joy.
- Our faith in God, has helped us endure his world.

While overcoming the traps, tricks and lies of the dark angel. We're ready to join God, and loved ones on the other side. But until our day comes and, our life on this side is over! We continue, to enjoy every minute, day and season in life.

God gives us on this side, until the last season in our life arrives!

Forever

In a reply to my sister Stephanie email, I used the word "Forever" for the first time in years. I used it after thanking her for her time and, efforts concerning my burial plot. Our mother told us growing up, "She would purchase burial insurance, until we became twenty-one!" After that we were responsibility for our own insurance and burial plot. After I turned twenty-one, I remember our mother saying "Baby your mother has somewhere to go on this side! It's time for you to choose a resting place!" After our mother passed away July17, 2009,

I understood the full meaning of her loving words.

The e-mail from Stephanie confirmed, the final paperwork for my burial plot beside our parents was completed. With tears filling my eyes, I thought about our mother's loving statements. I thought about the time, memories and, years. I spent playing football and, traveling across the country. I thought about all the years, I spent away from the family which truly loved me.

In my youth forever was a long time, it seemed immeasurable like a road without an end. Forever and, time were like a journey without a final destination. Forever was as large as an ocean and, as endless as the sky. As a teenager I feared nothing, even death was a friend.

But over the past thirty-seven years, that God has blessed me to live. The time and, forever I knew as a teenager have changed. Time was once absent and, missing. But, now it's a clock ticking away the years in my life. In my youth, time was like a road without an end. But as time has passes, the end of my road has gotten closer. In my youth forever was a journey without a destination. I realize now, I have to purchase an earthly resting place for my body.

Time and, forever were once as enormous as an ocean. But over time, it have diminished to a small burial plot. The time I knew in my youth, was as big as an open sky. But now it, can be measure it in square feet. After the death of my mother, my friend death returned to my life as an enemy. While fighting, against my enemy present in my life. I remembered the faith and, wisdom my parents taught me as a children.

They taught me, "I have to accept and embrace, the things in life that I fear or hate". They remind me, they're a part of our life until we leave his world!" Because of God love and, their teaching, I no longer look forward at death with fear or anger. While replying to my sister's e-mail I begin to cry.

Like our loving mother, I didn't cry:

- Tears of pain or fear.
- Tears of sadness or anger.
- They were tears of joy!

My joy was in knowing, at the end of my journey on this side. My body will rest beside our parents forever! My tears of joy were from listening to our mother loving words. By reserving my earthly location on this side. When my life on this side ends, my body will rest in the fields, woods and mountains of Arkansas. When my day comes for me to leave, I will cry for the loved ones I must leave behind. I will cry for a life and world, that I have come to love. Our leaving this side will cause us, to be overcome with emotions.

We can't let our leaving cause us to:

- Fear the dreams and, goals we still have in life.
- Hate the people and, things of his world.
- Be angry with God will and, purpose in our life.

Our leaving is God's way of returning his spirit and, us back to heaven. We enjoy, the precious life God has given us.

By allowing our faith in God, to help us endure our journey. When we reach the last stage of our journey in life. We have to remove everyone and everything which torments us on this side. We have to prepare a place for our physical body to remain on this side. Before we start our journey to the other side, God's are angels are waiting beside his throne. To start, there journey toward us. When our time comes, his angel will touch our physical body. Which will release God's Holy Spirit and our soul from its physical temple. God's angel will take us and, his Holy Spirit back to heaven.

When we approach heaven, we hear our love ones welcoming voices. We will cry tears of sadness, for the loved ones we must leave behind. Our tears of sadness will turn into tears of joy for the family members we're about join. "Forever".

May the peace, joy and love of God.

Be with us, until we're on the other side! "Forever!"

Fading Away

What a beautiful life and, world God has blessed us to see and enjoy. We marvel at the beautiful creations in his oceans. The endless skies and universes he has created. We're shocked by the countless stars and, planets which surround us.

After seeing God's creations, we're like:

- A small droplet of water, in his enormous oceans.
- A single molecule, in God's enormous universes, stars and planets.
- A small seed, wedged in tall grass below an enormous mountain.

In God's world we're like a small leaf, in the middle of a huge orchard. To my surprise our pride and, stubbornness has somehow allowed us to overcome God's greatness. By judging God by our standards, like we made his world. We're like children, lost in the wilderness of his world! God's knowledge has allowed us, to reach other worlds. But we get lost in our own cities! Our pride has allowed us, to count and name God's stars. But we don't know how many there are. Our knowledge has allowed us to look at and, name God's plants and universes. But we still don't know, how many there are, or where they end.

Until we totally surrender to God, our pride fights with his will and purpose in our life. His heavenly clock blesses us, by keeps track of our time on our journey. God starts his heavenly clock, the day we're born. His clock doesn't have minute or second hands. It doesn't have number, symbols or seasonal diagrams or pictures. God's heavenly clock, operate on his mercy, grace and love for us. We know from God holy word, our life and soul will fade away from this world. Each day God bless us to wake-up, he renews his love and mercy for us by allowing our earthly clock to keep running. After God renews his love for us, he removes a day from our earthly clock on this side. The day he removes from this side, is added to our heavenly clock.

When changes occurs to our face, body and age. They're signs our physical life on this side is starting to fade away. When god allows our earthly clock to count down our final days on this side. God will allow:

- His mountains, trees, and the stars to remain.
- His rivers, oceans and seas to stay.
- The clocks of our new generation and, our loved to continue running.

The physical body, which God blessed us to use on this side will remain on this side. Only his Holy Spirit and, our soul are allowed to cross over into heaven. God will bless our loved ones to look up at the stars and, think of us. After our life has faded way, our loved ones will thank God for our life on this side. The same way, we thanked him for our parents and loved ones life. After you finish reading my spiritual letters, you may want to know. "How do I know these things?

All I can tell you is, God revealed these things to me after "A Mother's Touch!"

Our mother's touch is as strong today. As it was four and a half years ago when it occurred. The essence of our life, will remain alive through our words, actions, pictures and faith.

For our family members and, the new generations to remember!

We Have to Think of Them as Sick!

I shared this statement with a co-worker, to help her deal with a conflict at work. I told her, "We have to think of some people as sick!" Their sickness could be:

- Emotional.
- Physiological.
- Medical.
- Spiritual.

Their sickness could be caused by drugs, or alcohol. Regardless of their sickness, God holds us responsible. For what we say and, how we treat them. After my statements my co-worker smiled and said, "That's what I needed to hear!" Given the situation, she decided to spoke to her supervisor. About the negative statements, made to her by another co-worker.

The same statements applies to our life, for the little while God blesses us to live. We have to deal with our sickness and, those of other people. And Yes! God does hold us responsible for what we say and, how we treat others. Because there sickness has made them weak, God has blessed our sickness to make us strong. God makes it the burden of the strong to help, endure, and tolerate those that are weak. Regardless of their words, actions or age.

They're rebellious sick children wanting attention, their way and love. Because of our rebellious life, God is our spiritual parent represented by the "Trinity". No! It want be easy to tolerate or help other. Nothing good or worth having is in life is easy. To have peace and joy in life, we help others that don't have peace or joy in their life.

As difficult as it is to accept we:

- Endure harmful words and, actions from family members and loved ones.
- Endure our pains, fears and insecurities of friends, co-workers and strangers.
- Embrace our pain, disappointments, failures and anger.

To receive our spiritual rewards, of peace and joy from God. We learn to love people spiritually, that hurt and deceive us. To the point of saying, "I did my best to help them!" Always remember, we're not alone in our efforts. God is in us, around us and, above us to help us during our challenges. So don't allow your emotions or efforts to control you. Because only God, Jesus and, the Holy Spirit gives the reward of peace and joy.

Don't think for a minute you have that power! Because you don't! Whatever power, wisdom or peace you have has been given to you by God. For his glory not for you pride to enjoy. Just do the best you can to help other without hurting yourself.

If God blesses us to do his will. We accept his will in our life and the lives of our loved ones!

Wherever you do, "Don't get in God's way!"

As the Sun Rises

While on vacation last week, I enjoyed a number of beautiful sun rises. One morning, while sitting inside my garage I looking out at the sun. The sunrise this morning looked bigger and, brighter than pass sun rises. This morning sun rise was so bright, it was like looking into the face of God. God's holiness is so bright, it's like looking into a hundred suns combined together. During this morning sun rise, I could feel the presence of God. In me, around me and above me. I could feel his power lifting his Holy Spirit and, my soul toward heaven. I felt God's spirit touching my thoughts, heart and soul.

I could feel the Holy Spirit saying "Your mother loves and misses you also! But she doesn't want to return to this side!" During that moment, I felt like a child for the first time in years. After the Holy Spirit touched me, years seem to turn into seconds. I felt like a child, looking through the eyes of a fifty-four year old man. In his own way, God was letting me know he has been with me. Throughout all the sunrises in my life. For whatever reason, he chose this moment and, time to let me know. Before realizing it, another thought about our loving mother touched my heart. During that moment my heart and soul cried out.

To:

- See the face.
- Hear the voice.
- Feel the touch.

The bright light of the sun, was like a wall. It was preventing me from seeing her face, hearing he voice or feeling her touch. But the bright light of the sun can't stop me from, remembering her face and, the sound of her voice. I could still feel her loving touch and, the essence of her love through the Holy Spirit. Suddenly, the bright wall of light reviled a spiritual gate. To God, my mother and, my love one on the other side. Hidden from our physical eye, the sun reviled a spiritual gate to the other side.

When the sun rises and, sets. We witness God's holiness and, a spiritual gateway to heaven. When we travel toward God's spiritual gates, our words and, actions will travelled ahead of us. This is why we learn to control our words and actions. By not allowing, evil people in darkness to block our path to God's sunlight, of joy and love. While the sunlight of God's love still rises and, sets in our life. We take joy in knowing we're journeying toward a holy gateway. We only have a "Little while" before we reach the gates of heaven. In our little while on this side, we do God's will.

We enjoy every sun rise and, sun set God blesses us to see. We know God's rewards of eternal life, can't be truly seen or felt on this side. Our faith helps us travel in peace and, joy.

We know the road ahead is blessed and, paved with God's grace, mercies and love.

As the Years Pass

As the years pass, I feeling the aches and pains of life. In my body trying to overtake my spirit and life. The nine years of playing football in middle school, high school and college football. Has left behind strained muscles in my fingers, arms and legs. The numerous car and, work accidents are like heavy chains wrapped around my body. Years of gaining and, losing weight has left me shirts and pant of different sizes. Because of my medical and, dental issues I remember telling my wife. "It's a good thing, I am not a horse!" Because you would putting me to sleep or sailing me.

Senior citizens say, getting older is a blessing and a curse. The blessings are from the years, God has allowed us to live. The curse is knowing our mind and, body can't do what they once did. My years of pain has left my body in the ICU under the care of the "Trinity" love.

As the years pass, I realize:

- My river of youth is now a tinkering stream.
- My ocean of knowledge is a small pond.
- My childish face is old and aged.

The body I enjoyed in my youth, has become weak, wrinkled and old. My mind, which was once filled with ideas, goals and dreams. Is on life support and being monitored by Jesus's love. For all we have lost and, are losing in life. God's spirit of love for us is the same today, as it was in our youth. Our physical years, will never age God's grace, mercy or love. Time can't age the Holy Spirit comfort, wisdom or holiness. Based on our faith the Holy Spirit and, time will shape us in God's holiness.

As we travel through life, we know a holy God:

- Walks beside us.
- Holy Spirit is inside us.
- Son's blood covers our mistakes and sins.

We go forward in life knowing, a joyous end is ahead of us. My loving mother would tell you, "Baby, your mother has somewhere to go on this side! It's time for you to choose a resting place!" We have both a earthly and, heavenly resting place we need to prepare for!

So if we must worry about something.

We should start worrying about our resting places!

I Didn't Need It Anyway!

When I think about my first car. I remember my wants and, the problems they created. I remember that 1970 Dodge Charger,

I wanted as a teenager. It had two air intake vent on the hood and, fifty inch racing wheels on the back tires. After looking at the car with my parents. I remember my mother's facial expressions saying, "I don't think so son, you want be getting that car!"

I remember her beautiful smile, when I purchased a 1966 Ford Mustang. Our father's facial expressions turned to pain, after he found out the car needed a new transmission. The replacement cost of the new transmission, was equal to the price I paid for the car. My father talking to the man, who sold me the car. He refused to refund my money and, take the car back. After our father took a depth breath, he shook his head and looked at me he said. "Now you know for yourself! Now that you've experienced it for yourself, no one has to tell you what mistake you made!"

Thinking back, I didn't need that fast racing car anyway. But I realize later, even the safe car had problems which I didn't check. This is one of the problems with our wants, many times when we receive them we're still not happy. We either don't want it, don't need it or, it has so many problems it's not worst it! Looking back at that 1970 Dodge Charger, I have no doubt at eighteen years old. I would have attempted to go the maximum speed on the speedometer. Who knows, I could have had a car accident and been killed! Realizing I could have been killed in a car accident. That new transmission wasn't a bad investment.

The same is true in life, our wants only seek to frustrate us. When God fulfills our needs, we are at peace and have joy. Our wants are like a bottle less pit, but our needs could fill a glass. Our wants will grow to the size of a mountain. While our needs are the size of an ant hill. Our wants could grow to the size of the moon, but our needs can fit into the palms of our hands. Our wants can make us a prisoner, to our standards and those of God's world. We can't allow our wants, to control our life. The dark angel waits for us, in the darkness of our wants, confusion and frustrations.

The dark angel hides:

- In darkness of our frustrations, desires and greed for the things of God's world.
- In darkness waiting for pain, loneliness, and suffering to weaken our faith.
- In darkness waiting for us to leave the light of God's love and holiness.

He waits in the darkness, away from God's light of truth, righ- teousness and love. After making our decisions about our wants and needs, we find our self asking "God to help me!" Why do we wait until after our decisions is made to call on God? When darkness is about to consuming our spirit and life. Why don't we ask and, allow God time to help us? But No! We're grown man and, women able to make our own decisions. Then when it comes time to pay the consequences for our decisions. We run to God and, others crying like a baby. Talking about, Why me? What did I do?

Allow me to help you, with my father words, "Now you know it for yourself! Now that you've made the decisions and experienced it for yourself, no one has to tell you what mistake you made!" If we don't ask God, his Holy Spirit, or one of his spirit vessels for help. We choose to be doomed to a life of pain and suffering. Keep letting your pride and, independent tell you. You're a mature adult able to make our own decisions.

I remember something in the bible about, "Pride going before destruction!" Let me know how that turns out for you! If you keep doing it your way, you'll find yourself saying, "If I hadn't only! I should have! Why didn't I?" This is my favorite statement from my youth. "I didn't need it! Or, I didn't want it anyway!"

As we journey we should ask God, to help us reject our wants. By accepting his spiritual needs for our life!

Special "Thanks" to Lisa

Lisa is my neighbor, and my classmate. She honored our mother by writing a short poem, for our mothers' funeral services.

My Neighbor, My Mother, My Friend you always had a kind word to say, When I was in my darkest days... Always smiling a Beautiful smile, When you rang my door bell, You brought food, you brought clothes,

And your kind words brought a whole lot more. My Neighbor—My Mother—My Friend The talk we had took me from feeling sad about it... To feeling good about it...

Encouraging me to hang in there... God puts on Me What I can Bare...

Saying everything will be alright... and it was. My Neighbor—My Mother—My Friend Over the years my Mother would say to us;

God couldn't have given us a better neighbor... Mrs. Theus My Neighbor—My Mother—My Friend Lisa

What You Should Know!

Kashawn, I am writing into words. What your Aunt Tina has already told you many times in person. But you were always moving too fast to listen. Or, you're just too stubborn to care. When you begin to experience your life as a women. Remember where you come from and the people that helped and loved you. Remembering your loved ones will helps you become grateful. When you couldn't achieve your wants, your parents and Aunt Tina were there to help you. They disciplined you when you were wrong and helped you when you were hurt, sad or upset.

Now that your mother and, loved ones are gone. You should always keep their memory in your thoughts and heart. Just because they're gone you can't and shouldn't forget what they taught you. You have no reason to blame God, for calling them home to heaven. Always remember God's thoughts and, ways are higher than our thoughts and ways. When our life end on this side, we'll stand before him for judgment. God want have to stand before us for our judgment.

Even if you didn't want it! Don't like it! Or can't accept it! Your love ones have returned to heaven. So stop dishonoring their memory with bad words, actions and behaviors.

What should you do?

- Be your best in life.
- Remember your mistakes.
- Accept responsibility for your decisions, words and actions.
- Ask God to help you daily.

Why should you accept responsibility for you actions? Because you keep saying, you've reached the door to womanhood. But you can't pass through the door of womanhood acting like a child. You say you're at the door of wisdom. But you can't go through that door, making the same mistakes over and over again. You keep saying you're at the door of knowledge. Ok, you should already know that everything that looks good and feel good isn't always good for you. Because of your experiences in life, no one has to keep telling you the right things to do. You're an intelligent young women allow your knowledge to help you, rather than hurt you. Life is a learning process, so stop thinking you know everything about life. Tina told you about your words and actions years ago when you were a teenager. If she's still telling you, the same thing ten years later. You didn't listen the first time or you like doing things your way. After all you've been through the past five years. Stop and, take a look at your words, actions and life. No one has to tell you, what you've been through!

You already know! So let the pains and, mistakes of your past help you become a stronger woman.

You need to look at?

- Your decisions and, not your excuses.
- Your actions, rather than your justifications.
- Your behavior and, blame yourself for your life being the way it is!

When you look back at your past, stop and remember the loved ones that loved and helped you. Remember how their words and, actions helped give you understanding and wisdom. Their words not yours! Gave you direction in your life, their words of faith taught you how to have faith in a loving God.

Lastly, remember the family members that helped you financially. Only to see you waste your money, on people that don't care or love you. Take care of your sons, Kayden and Noah. If you don't take care of your sons, their childhood memories will remind you of your selfish actions and broken promises.

When they become adults and, tell you about their childhood. Their memories will bring tears of pain to your eyes and heart. You will look back remembering:

- The deceitful friends, you put before you family.
- The shame you felt when you deceived your son's and, family members.
- The lies you told to get what you wanted.

When you look back, you should remember what getting your way got you. I hope and, pray you look back quickly and honestly. Look back now while you're still young and let your understanding help you. When you're young, time is a wonderful friend but when you become an adult time turn into an enemy.

Because you're at the door of womanhood:

- Your past decisions, actions and mistakes are the path you chose in life.
- Not repeating your past, prevents you from making the same mistakes in your future.
- Your present is becoming your future life.

After making your decisions as a woman, learn to accept the consequences for your decisions. Let your consequences help you grow and, develop into a strong Christian woman. Ask God to help you with decisions before you make them.

Your loved ones will only be here for "A little while" to help you on your journey!"

After they help you, when the time comes learn to help them in return!

Only God knows how long he'll bless us to be here! I Love you, Uncle Waldo

Come on Now!

I n my childhood, I developed a speech problem. My tongue
couldn't keep up with my thoughts or words. I knew what I
was saying but, no one else could understand me. I was frustrated
with my family member for not being able to understanding me.
My childhood speech problems frustration me for years, until I
received professional help.

In Paul's letter to the church at Corinthians, he speaks to church
members about moving from childhood to adulthood.

"When I was a child, I talked like a child, I thought like a child,
I reasoned like a child. But, when I became a man, I put a way
childish thing." (1 Corinthians 13:11 NIV)

When I look around and see mature adults speaking and, acting
like children. All I can say is "Come on now! "From there words
and actions they appear to be emotionally and, mentally struck in
their childhood. We can't just focus on them, we need to look at
our self first to see the cause of our problem "us". By truthfully
examining our self we begin, to reach toward a spiritual turning
point in our life. We can't keep using other people as excuses. We
have to learn to stop saying you, he, they and them. We need to

start saying, I, me and us. Why would we want to copy the negative behaviors of people that reject us and God?

If we know someone is a liar. We can't allow their words and lies to upset us. When people criticize us for no reason, don't allow their words of hatred and jealousy make you angry. We have to remind our self, "They're sick!" We tell our self, "They're during the best they can!" Even if they're not doing their best! We can't let them or our self stop us from being our best! We can't allow their deceitful words and, lies to hurt or stop us. When they do everything in their power to cause us pain. They're not our friends beloved, "They're sick!" They have chosen to be unhappy and, they want us to be the same way. When our paths cross these, "Sick spirits".

We have to, ask God to help us:

- Pray for them and our self.
- Forgive them and us for our sins.
- Heal there spirit and ours.

We allow God's will to be done in our life and there's. Because God may allow them to remain children. Until they choose his wisdom and love. He may leave them in darkness. Until they repent and, ask for his grace and mercy in their life. He may allow their spiritual sickness to torment them. So don't wait time caring for "Sick spirits" that don't want God or our help in their life. When we learn to do God's will, we put them in "God's Holy hands!" We do this by removing them from "Our Hands!"

God has millions of spiritual vessels to help them and, us on our journey. When we do what God has ask us to do, we pray for our self and those we love. We let the blessing of God's grace and, mercy guide us and them to his light of love. If we do too much, we interfere with God's will and, purpose for their life. We may deceive our self by thinking God needs our help! "Come on now!"

We already know:

- God doesn't need, our help with his decisions.
- God will use us and, them as an instrument of his mercy, love and power.
- God is the master of our life, if our faith chooses his will and, purpose for our life.

We ask God to allow us to be a blessing to others, by being an instrument of your will and love.

When we do this, we want let our will be done!

Beautiful People

While enjoying life, I think about all the beautiful people I've met in my life. I am not talking about their facial or physical appearance. I remember them because of their spiritual beautiful. My wife Tina, has the same spiritual beautiful as my mother during her life. The spiritual beautiful God gave them is like an angel. Their spirit of love was so pure it's like fresh fruit on a tree. Because of God, my parents and love ones always had a spiritual beautiful in their lives. Time may fade their words, from our thoughts. It may remove their touch from our life. But there spiritual beautiful is remembered in my heart. There photographs are visual evidence of their beautiful spirit while they were with us.

Time or there leaving can't fade the beauty of their:

- Belief in God's love.
- Hope in God's word.
- Faith and love for God in their life.

Time will never fade their words of faith and praise to God. Their beautiful spirit will remains in our thought and memories forever. The standards of God's world look at the physical appearance of our temple. But God looks at the heart and soul inside his temple.

I wrote this spiritual letter to my family and, loved that seek beauty. Do what you must, to enhance your exterior temple. But, don't forget where your true beauty comes from. If you become distracted by the physically beautiful of people around you. Look up and thank God for your health. Thank him for a sound mind and a soul filled with the peace and joy of the Holy Spirit. When we feel no one loves us because of your physical appearance. Look up again and thank God for your sight, understanding, wisdom and his love. When we surrender to God we're never alone. Because, God is always in us, around us and above us! If we don't sense God's presence in your life.

It maybe because we're distracted by our insecurities and the world's opinion of how you should look.

God helps us see the beauty of his grace, mercy and love in our life.

Why Stay?

This spiritual letter is written in the memory of my loving cousin Diane. She passed away May 2012 from a heart attack. I wrote this spiritual letter to Diane, because of her spiritual beautiful, heart and soul. When we remember the loved ones who have left this side, to be with God. We begin to asking our self, "Why do I want to stay here?" When their memories and, loss touches our thoughts, hearts and soul. We look up toward heaven and ask God, "Why do I want to stay in your world?" When I remember their smiles, laughter and their love of life. We look up to heaven and ask our family members and loved ones, "Why should I stay on this side without you?"

When their birthdays and, anniversaries arrives. We're forced to accept their loving memories with joy and pain. Looking around at the loved ones beside us, helps us answer our question. We stay to enjoy life and enjoy the family members and loved ones still on this side. Each morning when I look into the mirror, I ask our self.

How long will God bless me to live? Forever!

No! Beloved! That's not an option on this side. Even if it was an option! Why would you want to burden our loved ones or a friend with caring for us. Why would we want to stay in God's world? Not knowing who we are or where we are! If we're in this state of mind, we're not living we're prisoners to our mind, body and life. We struggle daily against death, while enjoying whatever happiness we can acquire on this side. We struggle with time and our aging body to enjoy our life and the remaining years ahead. We struggle against a life filled with challenges and pains, to receive a few earthly rewards.

While trying to understand God's will and purpose in our life. We have to stay on this side, because God has work for us to do! In our struggles we may become angry with God, and question his purpose for our life. We find ourselves asking God, with all the beautiful people and things you bless me to enjoy on this side. Why do you take away the loved ones, which are our earthly treasures in life? The loss of our loved ones is God's ways of letting us know, this world isn't our home. God knows we have come to love and treasures our loved ones and our life in his world. But, our love of God's earthly treasures separates us from him and heaven. Because of our separation from God, he uses death to return us and his Holy Spirit back to heaven.

God knows if we lose the people:

- That gave us joy and happiness on this side.
- We want desire to stay on this side.
- Our love for those we love helps prepare us to leave this side.

In his loving way God lets us know he's calling us home to an eternal life. So we have to learn to enjoy every day, person and thing we experience on this side. Regardless of what's going on in us and around us.

The main themes of this spiritual letters and my book is to:

- Enjoy the life which God has given us.
- Ask God to remove everything which torment us in life.
- Don't let anyone or anything stop you from enjoying life.
- Don't let anyone block your path to God, heaven and our loved ones in heaven.

Take joy in our little while on this side, and then truthfully ask yourself.

"Do I really want to stay on this side for eternity?" I don't think so!

What Happened to the Light?

After living in the darkness of our emotions, sin and God's world.

We find ourselves asking, "What happened to the light?" I am not talking about physical light which helps us to see. I am talking about the light of the Holy Spirit which helps us to live.

Without the Holy Spirit we feel alone without:

- Hope or love.
- Joy or happiness.
- Faith or God's mercy.

Without the light of the Holy Spirit we're feel alone. Even if we're surrounded by our families and hundreds of people. When these times, feelings and storms come into our life. Don't waste time looking down or at our self. Because all we'll found there are our failures, pride, selfness and sins waiting for us to pick them up. The light of God's Holy Spirit is waiting on us to let it shine. It's already with us on our journey, which is God's and its temple.

The darkness which surrounds our life is in our:

- Thoughts caused by our pride and sins.
- Heart caused by our pride, greed and the treasures of this world.
- Soul caused by our lack of faith and truth in God to accept our sins.

We realize our problems and the solutions are both within us. So stop asking "What happened to the light?" Nothing happened to the light! We stop embracing the light and our faith in God. We started embracing our faith in our pride, knowledge and our desires for the things of God's world. Our knowledge and pride deceives us, into thinking we have the power to control our life. Then when the storms and trails of life start to overwhelm us we don't understand, "Why we can't change or stop it?"

We ask our self, "Why can't my thoughts, efforts and experiences help me?" We realize too late that our pride and self-will gets us into these situations. But, they don't have the power to get us out. Before the storms and problems in life overtake us. We have to realize our solution is to surrender our life to God's will and purpose. We can choose to be a victim of our problems or a servant of God's. For us to serve God we must pray, repent and ask his Holy Spirit to help us surrender to God.

"If my people, which are called by my name, shall humble themselves, and pray, and seek my face, and turn from their wicked ways; then will I hear from heaven, and will forgive their sin and heal their land." (2 Chronicles 7:14, NIV)

God continually ask us to turn from the darkness of our prideful and sinful life. Back to his love, the light of his Holy Spirit and the blood of Jesus. What we need to do now is to ask our self, "Why haven't I did it?"

We should find peace and stop fighting by knowing our ways

caused us pain, shame and regret. God's love for us, can bless us to become masters over all he has created.

I pray to God:

"We allow the Holy Spirit to bring its light and, God's holiness back into our life!"

Why Do My Steps
Cause Me to Fall?

It's easy to look around and find people and, things to blame. For our words, actions, and failures in life. We look at everyone and everything but our self. Because we don't want to see the true source of our problem "us". God stills blesses us to exist and enjoy our life in his world, for a little while. We can't continually waste time falling and getting up. When we look back at our path through the years. No one has to tell us what we said, did or where we have been in our life. "If my thoughts and words become inconsistent with my actions. Then I am lying and deceiving myself!" I continually use these statements to help me examine my words and action. When we struggle with our self, God has allowed our:

- Body to have strength
- Brain to reason answers.
- Soul to rejoice in our faith.

God us our pains and troubles to become stepping stones to his forgiveness, mercy and love. "For our little while in my life!"

We should learn to allow God's Holy Spirit to speak for us. To guide our steps and, help us endure storms. Which are waiting to plague and destroy our life. If we allow him, God will allow our mistakes to be a tool for our change. Rather than a tool, used for my destruction. My prayer, "When I got sick and tired of myself! Was to ask, God to take my will, pride and life and do with me as he will. While I suffer on this side, allow my soul to soar with your Holy Spirit above my problems, sins and pain. Until, I return to you and my love ones in heaven.

For us to receive God's spiritual gifts we must:

- Talk using God's holy words.
- Walk in God's holy footsteps.
- Act and behave like God.

When we do these things, and we can! Beloved! We want keep asking, What happened to the light:

- We want continually stumble and, fall in life.
- We want allow our darkness or any darkness to cover his Holy Spirit.
- We want keep apologize to God and, our loved ones for our words or actions.

When we do what God has ask us to do, we free the Holy Spirit and our soul.

After we're free we journey through life with:

- Faith in our thoughts.
- Joy in our heart.
- Praise for God on our lips and in our soul.

When we travel in God's holy footsteps, we enjoy the beauty of life without falling!

171

What Do We Do Now?

After the passing of our mother and love ones. I found myself asking, "What do I do now?" With another Thanksgiving and holiday season approaching. Their arrival doesn't have the joy it once did. Because the loved one we enjoyed during the holidays are no longer with us. Their memories are a past reflections, we graze at for a few second before it fades away. During this time of my life, I feel like I am going through rush hour traffic.

I start my journey saying goodbye to my wife, family and love ones. After I leave my home and enter my car. I ask God to help me make to my destination and back home safely. I start my journey by avoiding cars and truck on both sides of my street. While driving through my neighborhood, to the main road which will take me to the freeway. When I reach the freeway, I drive along the service road until I reach the ramp. Which allows me to merge with the oncoming freeway traffic. While driving safely to enter the freeway thee always another vehicle speeding down the slow lane. Which the ramp merge with to get on the freeway.

After entering the freeway, I begin to encounter the challenges. I will face on my journey to work and through life. After merging with the fast oncoming traffic, I find a small space to begin my journey. I am watchful of other drivers speeding down the freeway. Looking up the freeway, I see an accident caused by one of the speeding drivers. I pray for their safety and thank God for my safe journey.

I am tempted to go faster in hopes of getting ahead of the traffic before it backs up. I quickly realize the heavy traffic and numerous speeding drivers, want allow me to go faster. When I approach the accident I am forced to switch lanes or exit the freeway to detour around the accident and other drivers. The accident and detour may cause me to arrive at my destination late. With God's help I arrive to my destination safely. After work, church, shopping or visiting a loved ones. I say a short prayer before starting my journey back home. The route home may be different, from the one I traveled to reach my destination. I may encounter new obstacles and detours on my journey home. But I travel toward home with joy and faith in God. To arrive home safety I have to be focused, discipline and, determined to reach my destination.

I am distracted and frustrated by speeding drivers with beautiful cars and truck on their journey. I decided to avoid the freeway for a few minutes by pass through downtown. I see people of different races and spirits on their journey home. Many of them touch my heart with sadness, while others touches my thoughts with desires. I realize I can't do anything to help them or, reward my desires.

I ask God to help me and, them as we journey back to him. After driving a few minutes through downtown. I arrive back to the freeway which will take me home. I prepare for my journey home, with God's help and my faith. I enter the freeway happy knowing I am going home, regardless of the obstacles ahead God is with me.

We take the same type of journey, as we travel through life. After God blesses us to live a beautiful life, our goal should be to get home to heaven. Regardless of the obstacles, people, problems, detours, fears or accidents in our path. Our main desire and focus is to return to heaven. We don't waste time concerning ourselves with God's schedule. We can't do anything to change his schedule anyway! What do we do now? We continue to enjoy life and do God's will.

We know what will happens if we continue to do our will! Believe me, "You don't want to keep going there!" Don't keep asking, "What do I do now?" If you don't know after reading this book. Read it again and ask God to give you the answer. God, his son Jesus and his Holy Spirit are the only ones that can answer your question any.

If you truly want an answer, you'll have to wait on them to answer you!

At the End of Our Journey

When we reach the end of our journey. We'll look back remem- bering what we've said and did throughout our life. We'll remember the people we met and places we've traveled in life. We'll look backwards remembering all the mistakes we made, pains and consequences we've experienced and endured. We'll look at belief, truth and faith in God. We should only look back to learn from the mistakes which helped us grow! After we finish looking backwards we look forward. With a tears of joy and sadness in our eyes. We look forward, with a smile of happiness on our faces. Knowing the years ahead of us are counting down. We know our faith in God will heal our grief, pain, problems. We're filled with peace, after accepting we have what need from God and his world.

Time and God will never allow us to win our final battle over death. Our journey and battles on this side will continue. Until our time runs out and God calls us home to heaven. As our journey on this side continue, we'll see the beginning and end of days and years. Until our mind and body are touched by God's holy angel. While we remain on this side, we are forced to journey forward. We continue to do the things, which our life requires us to do.

To not do these things, places God's Holy Spirit and us in a dead temple. The Holy Spirit, which God has blessed to accompany us on our journey. Wants to return home to heaven with or without us. To not do what God has ask us to do. We dishonors his gift of life and, his Holy Spirit. We're wasting God's precious gift of life. By allowing our problems, evil spirits and the challenges of his world to be more powerful than God. If we're God's humble servant, we can't allow our self or his Holy Spirit to suffer. We can't allow anything or anyone in God's world to stop us in our journey. God want allow his Holy Spirit to dwell in our dead and unholy temple. We can't continually damaging and, destroying our life and think we're only hurting our self.

We have to stop thinking, and start believing God's:

- Holy word, is our path.
- Mercy and, grace are the forces which gives us hope and faith.
- Love, is what will help us reach heaven.

The loving memories of our parents and family members also helps us on our journey. If you're ask yourself, "What should I do?" The answer is simple, "We obey and have faith in God, by enjoying our families and life". We're preparing for a new life in heaven. Because all the things we earned and, received in God's world will return to his world. Time aging our bodies and minds, so don't keep worrying about how long we will live.

One thing is for sure, "It want be forever! So you can stop worrying about that!"

However long God blesses us to live is a blessing! Nothing on this side is enough or everlasting anyway! God has decided to give us, "A little while" to enjoy the life he has given us on this side. On this side our self-will is allowed to control our carnal thoughts and bodies. Our self-will rejects God will and purpose in our life.

It cling to the carnal life which God has given to us as a gift. We allow our carnal minds to block God's beautiful gift of life.

"No one can serve two masters. Either you will hate the one and love the other, or you will be devoted to the one and despise the other. You can't serve God and money (Matthew6:24 NIV)."

When we look back over our life, who does our words and actions say we have served. Don't try to be smart and say, "Myself"! Because your friend, was kicked out of heaven for doing the same thing! So we'll either be with our parents and loved ones in heaven.

Or, you'll be with your friends in hell, if that's your choice!

A Special Thank You!

This letter is a special thanks to Annette Barnett. She was a retiring claim department transcriptionist from my company. From the spiritual gifts which God's gave you. You help set free the words and thoughts in my book. Your time and, gifts allowed my thoughts and, word to live. While preparing for retirement you took time out of your schedule. To help me organize many of the e-mails, words and thought in my 'Mother's" book.

No amount of money can reward you for the time and help you gave to organize my book. Which honors my mother, family and loved ones memory.

I hope my small love offering and, a copy of my mother's completed book. Will let you know how much I appreciate your time, labors and talents.

I pray God continues to bless you, each day of your journey. Take care of yourself!

Waldo Theus

You Know!

You know the rewards of your job and, this world will never match the labors of your soul.

You know our true rewards, of our labors aren't based on the standards of God's world.

The true rewards of life is given to us from our faith in God's love. Your gift of love is a beautiful spirit which will never be forgotten.

Your faith and this book which you help create, will help us and others reach their eternal destination.

May God bless you and, your family on your journey and in your life.

I pray that you journey and, life be long! Written to you with spiritual love and respect, Waldo Theus

Scripture List

John11:1-45 (NIV) It's Better to Let Them GO!
Then to Let Then Suffer!

Roman8:23 (NIV) It's Better to Let Them GO!
Then to Let Then Suffer!

Matthew 10:16 (NIV) Crossing Over

1Corinthians 13:11 (NIV) Life Seasons
Come on Now

1Corinthians 13: 13 (NIV) Fear, Pain, Love

Chronicles 7:14 (NIV) What Happened to the light?

Matthew 10: 16 (NIV) At the End of our journey

Thank You to my Loved Ones!

To my wife Tina, my family and loved ones.
I joyfully journey with you, until our life on this side ends!

Printed in the United States
by Baker & Taylor Publisher Services